Dr Frank Barna
is a nuclear physicist who spent
his early career working at Britain's Atomic Weapons
Research Establishment. Since then he has become an
authority on weapons proliferation; the Guardian
newspaper of London describes him as "one of
Britain's most respected defence analysts".
In 1970 Dr Barnaby was appointed Director of the
Stockholm International Peace Institute (SIPRI), and he
was later made a Visiting Professor of universities in
Amsterdam and Minnesota. He is currently an
Honorary Research Fellow at King Alfred's College,
Winchester, in England.
In 1982 Dr Barnaby edited *The Nuclear Arms Race*.
His other books include: *The Invisible Bomb*, 1989; *The
Automated Battlefield*, 1987; *Star Wars*, 1987; *Future
Warfare*, 1986; and *Verification Technologies*, 1986.
In 1990 he was invited, with three other international
observers, to supervise the de-militarisation of one of
the world's most ruthless terrorist organisations, the
M-19 terrorists of Columbia.
Dr Barnaby lives in Hampshire, Southern England, with
his wife Wendy, a science writer and broadcaster; they
have two grown-up children.

Further reporting by
SIMON REEVE

VISION Paperbacks,
a division of
Satin Publications Limited
3 Neal Street
Covent Garden
London WC2H 9PU
Email: 100525.3062@compuserve.com

Cover design and layout: Justine Hounam.
Typesetting and design: Pixel Press.
Printed and bound in Great Britain: The Bath Press, Bath.

©1996 Dr Frank Barnaby/VISION Paperbacks
ISBN: 1-901250-01-6

VISION Paperbacks

Dr Frank Barnaby

INSTRUMENTS OF TERROR

Mass Destruction Has Never Been So Easy...

Contents

Illustrations

x

Introduction

Terrorism has now reached epidemic proportions in many parts of the world and the opportunities to cause mass suffering are getting ever easier. The threat posed by terrorists touches all our lives and looks set to continue for many years. Even though a few terrorists still blow themselves up trying to plant their own home-made devices and others are captured by police, there are always volunteers prepared to take their place.

This book looks at how democracies are under threat from increasingly resourceful terrorist groups and shows how more and more people are dying from the bullet and the bomb. No country can feel safe, and being a beneficent democracy is no protection.

Counter-terrorism measures can, of course, help but the determined bomber or gunman can usually devise a way of attacking a target. Their task is made easy because, more often than not, the victims are innocent people, unaware of the need to be vigilant.

As this book went to press, British politicians and representatives of terrorists were still talking about talks as the 'troubles' in Northern Ireland continued. The conflict in that small area of north-western Europe might seem intractable, but perhaps I can begin with a personal story, one of hope and an object lesson for

others. It concerns a once active Colombian terrorist group called M-19 who had a frightening history of bloodshed.

M-19 points up some of the trends in terrorism which this book attempts to analyse. It had a political aim but was also enmeshed in organised crime. However, on March 9, 1990, it signed a peace treaty with the Colombian government and gave up its war.

This happened partly as a result of the Colombian government offering M-19 members an amnesty, except for one terrorist called Clara Enciso - the only survivor of an attack on the Palace of Justice in Bogota - one of the worst terrorist atrocities ever carried out.

That attack happened on November 6, 1985 when M-19 fighters invaded the Justice building with more than 300 people inside. They were all taken hostage and the Colombian army began a battle to release them. The building caught fire and many hostages were executed by the terrorists. At least 115 people died, including 11 out of 24 Supreme Court judges.

The peace treaty was all the more remarkable given that back-ground and the hatred it engendered in the Colombian population. However, because of the commitment of a few brave individuals progress was made. To emphasise the fact that M-19 was not surrendering to the government, but was giving up its armed strug-gle voluntarily, the group insisted on its weapons being handed over to an independent commission consisting of four international observers - one of which was myself.

In a tense atmosphere deep in the Colombian mountains, the weapons were handed over to us at the two main M-19 terrorist bases. Each weapon was handed to a commission member and we checked it against an inventory agreed between M-19 and the Colombian government. All the weapons were then transported by air under our strict supervision to a foundry in the Colombian city of Cali and melted down.

The exercise was a remarkable sight to witness and left a deep impression on me. It was also highly educational and showed me for the first time the full extent of a modern terrorist arsenal. There

were approximately 700 active fighters within M-19, and the group had a modern military communications system and kept their records on computer. They were also exceedingly well armed, with weapons obtained from Libya, Nicaragua, and Cuba.

Their arsenal consisted of light and heavy machine guns (including Uzis and Brownings: 50 and 30 calibre), terrifying assault rifles (AR-15, Galil, FAL, and M-16's), carbines, shotguns, pistols (including the Browning high-power 9-mm automatic), revolvers, and explosives (including plastic explosives).

The M-19 group were formed in 1970 in reaction to alleged fraud in the Presidential elections of April 19 (M-19 means the April 19th Movement). Its ideology is hard to classify but is perhaps best described as nationalist. However the other observers and I soon learnt that to raise money, M-19 maintained close relations with Colombia's drug traffickers and the big drug barons, including those in the infamous Medellin Cartel. For some time it controlled cocaine production in many areas until the plantations were destroyed by government forces. Taxing peasants growing coca, in return for providing protection against attacks by police and the army, was the main source of M-19's finances.

Others were ransoms from kidnapping land-owners and the executives of foreign companies, extortion, and providing security services in areas in which Colombia's big drug barons operated. The group raised millions of dollars a year in this way.

The Colombian government could not have achieved a military victory over M-19 and the group was by no means beaten when it gave up terrorism. In fact, it controlled large rural areas where it was the only authority and provided social services such as educating children, helping farmers, providing medical services, as well as offering security and a semblance of law and order.

In these areas it was reasonably popular. So why did its leaders decide to give up the armed struggle? They claimed to be fighting for a more even distribution of wealth in Colombian society and to make more opportunities available to poorer people through education, improved health services, and so on. They decided they

had achieved all they could through violence and were convinced they could in future best achieve their aims through the political process.

On March 10, 1990, immediately after its truce with the government, M-19 participated in national elections to elect a new Congress and in local and regional elections as a legal political party. It did much better in these elections than most commentators had forecast. M-19's extraordinarily charismatic leader, Carlos Pizzara Leon-Gomez won 10 per cent of the votes in the election for the mayor of Bogota. He then became the Presidential candidate but was assassinated during the campaign.

His place was taken by another former M-19 leader, Antonio Navarro Wolf, who won a respectable 13 per cent of the vote and the party won 22 congressional seats. In the 1994 Presidential elections Antonio Navarro came third with 3.8 per cent of the vote, a sharp loss since the 1990 election. In the 1994 election the M-19 party lost 21 of its 22 seats in Congress.

These disappointing results, internal divisions, and poor leadership have left M-19 in some confusion. Only time will tell whether or not it can recover its former strength, but M-19s renunciation of violence was a courageous act. All of the ex-members of M-19 faced many threats - from right-wing death squads, from members of other guerrilla groups who objected to M-19 giving up its arms, from more extreme M-19 members who did not trust the government to keep their part of the peace bargain, and the drug gangs who wanted to settle old scores.

As part of the peace agreement M-19 was protected by government security forces, and presumably still are. They were given the same protection as government ministers. But this protection was of limited value, as proved by the assassination of Pizzaro, and of many other political figures.

The rank and file members of M-19 were less keen on demobilisation than were the leaders. Some of them had been professional terrorists for many years and they faced an uncertain future. Settling back into civilian life, often in poor rural areas, was, to say

the least, not easy. The government was rightly pleased with its peace agreement with M-19 and has tried hard to make similar agreements with other Colombian terrorists and guerrilla groups. But peace talks have not been successful and conflict has killed some 30,000 people since the mid-1960s.

The disarmament of M-19 was an important event because it brought to an end an armed conflict and strengthened democracy in Colombia. Standing in the jungle amid some of the world's most dangerous terrorists I could not help hoping that the initiative had a significance beyond the shores of Colombia, and that it provided a crucial blueprint for other future bilateral peace processes between governments and those who wage terror.

However in the years since that agreement was signed, the world has witnessed a fundamental shift in the nature of terrorism. Groups such as M-19 have become less significant and have been demoted in the 'league-table' of murderous groups by a new breed of terrorist who has few aims but who wants to inflict maximum destruction on the world. In the post-Cold War era, we are faced by terrorists with no moral compunctions preventing them from undertaking mass killings and with access to many new means of committing atrocities. This book is an attempt to investigate and warn of the dangers posed by these groups, and the terrible risk they will obtain weapons of mass destruction.

Chapter One

DIRTY TRICKS

The first tentative meeting took place in the Europa Hotel, Belfast, one of the most bombed buildings in the world. Donald was a back-room boy - a maker of ingenious lethal explosive devices. He had agreed to discuss the possibility of telling the story of how he became an expert in this grizzly profession. The meetings continued on mainland Britain where he finally felt confident to speak more openly. He spoke in matter-of-fact tones - like a worker in a car plant telling how he puts an engine together. This is the story of an IRA bomb-maker.

"The IRA is proud of its achievements," Donald* boasted. "In the last century we not only invented the time-bomb but also the first submarine. Republicans are adapters of what ever is at hand. The simple way is the best."

"The first time-bomb was like that," he continued. "They took a box full of gun powder, fixed on to it was a time-clock and a pistol with its barrel pointing into the explosive. A string wound round the hands of the clock and was tied to the pistol's trigger. As the hands went round, the string tightened and the gun went off. It was crude but it worked. One blew up Scotland Yard in the 1890s."

"After that it was easy," he said. "Nearly all the components for bombs can be bought over the counter. The hardest thing is explosives but those can also be made.

Not his real name.

"Ireland has lots of farms, land means crops and crops mean fertiliser. That is what we used - it is called Co-op mix because we got it from the local co-operative."

"Fertiliser is made of nitrate and that is the base of most explosives the Republicans use. You get a pan, grind the fertiliser into dust in a food blender, put some water and heat . . . [further crucial details have been omitted] . . . it sounds easy but the Republican role of honour shows that it was not. In the 1970s, the IRA lost more volunteers to Co-op mix-making than they did to the forces of the

state and loyalism. "Death was usually caused when preparing the mix in tin baths or aluminium pots. It reacted to the metal sometimes and blew up. When it was dried, it was bagged and ready for use as a booster charge. The primary charge was usually some commercial explosive like Franjex or Semtex. We experimented with fulminate of mercury as a home-made detonator but it was usually better to get commercial ones.

"Have you heard the joke about Mickey Mouse and Big Ben joining the IRA?" asked Donald. "We made TPUs - timing power units with Micky Mouse watches and Big Ben 'Westclox' alarm clocks because they had a plastic face which was an insulator. That meant you could screw a metal contact into them which completed an electrical circuit when it hit one of the hands. We would drill a hole in the face and use a matchstick to jam the hand until we wanted to set the clock going."

Donald described how this was superceded by a design using kitchen clock timers, or a device called a 'Memopark', bought on the Continent. This was a tiny clock which could be wound up to run for an hour. Its name stemmed from the fact that its purpose was to tell car-drivers when their time on a parking meter was running out. However, it made an ideal bomb timer as the device had a dial which slowly revolved. This would operate a switch passing electricity from a battery to a detonator."

Donald bemoaned the fact that electronic timers in modern video machines were no longer as useful as older models. "The timers can be used to delay an explosion for a month. That's what they used in the bomb that blew up Thatcher and the Tory government in the Grand Hotel, Brighton. The timers in the older video machines could be worked off a battery but after the bombing they changed the design. You have to expect them to do things like that."

Donald said that by the early 1970s, bomb-makers were getting more sophisticated and learning how to shape explosive charges: "The idea was to send the blast in a particular direction. Explosives are lazy - they will always blow out at the point of lowest resistance, so we could hide cone shaped charges in a van or a car, directed to

explode with greatest force at the target.

"If you remember the Bishopsgate bombing [in London], there was a bloody great hole in the road beneath where the bomb went off. That was to destroy telephone and computer cables buried beneath the street."

"From the start of the War, home-made landmines or claymores were used in rural areas of Ulster. Active service units would keep roads under observation for army patrols while IRA technical officers would search for culverts channelling streams under the road. These would be packed with charges and detonated when the patrol passed above. Often they would be set off by a long electrical wire that lead across the border into the Irish Republic.

"You needed quite a large current of electricity from that distance and car batteries would be used, connected to a simple door bell push-button. Some ATOs would add another light switch in the circuit to make it doubly safe.

"The best training manual we ever had was the Ladybird book for children called "Batteries, Bulbs and Magnets", said Donald. He went on to explain how two of his former friends, Dominic McGlinchy (who was shot dead in 1994) and Francis Hughes (who died in a prison hunger strike in 1981), read the book and came up with a new idea.

"It helped them to invent the most potent booby trap device we had ever seen - using a clothes peg. The Ladybird book suggested using the peg to make a morse code key. Two thumb tacks were pushed into each end of the peg so that the spring brought them together. If wires were attached, it made a simple circuit breaker and we adapted it. By putting plastic attached to a line between the tacks, it stopped the current from flowing to a detonator. The line could be attached to a door so that when it was opened the plastic would be yanked out and the bomb would blow the victim to bits. One young soldier was killed when he picked up a copy of the sex magazine 'Men Only'. The line was attached to it.

"The clothes peg could also be used to booby trap a large bomb. For example milk churns were often used, packed with explosive. If

they were found, attempts would be made to take to them to bits but you could hide the peg attached to a secondary circuit in the centre of the explosive so that if it was pulled, the plastic separator would be pulled out and the bomb would be set off.

"You could also tie the line to the air-valve on the tyre of a car so that when the wheel turned round and the line tightened, a bomb under the passenger compartment attached by a magnet would go off. The uses of clothes pegs were endless.

"The INLA [another Republican terrorist group] perfected something using mercury switches, ripped out of the heating systems in the Divis Flats [in Ulster]. Airey Neave [a Conservative MP] died that way. As his car was driving up a ramp from the House of Commons car park, the switch tilted, the mercury, which was a liquid metal, flowed around two contacts sending electricity to the detonator. Cars might be driven around for days before they went up a hill that was steep enough to cause a detonation."

Donald said all these designs are still in use. "Did you see the photographs of the bombs they found in London recently [October 1996]. You could see the Memoparks, the design hasn't changed."

He said firebombs and blast incendiaries are commonly used because everything can be bought from local shops. "You get petrol, firelighters, soap and sugar, that sort of thing. We also used old-fashioned flash-bulbs as detonators, they worked well but they are now difficult to find. Russia is still a source. The IRA makes its own napalm with these sort of materials."

He said bomb factories were usually installed in someone's house. "Nowadays they are very high tech. Provo [IRA] engineers will hollow out the ground beneath the floor of a sympathiser's kitchen creating room for cookers, electric grinders and space to pack the Co-op mix. The police went to visit a friend of mine and there was no in. They opened the letter box to see if her boyfriend was there and became suspicious of the smell. They put in an explosive 'sniffer' - it went off the scale. They found one of the biggest halls of mix ever under the living room floor. She got ten years."

Donald disclosed that training of new recruits often takes place 'on the job' but there were also special camps in isolated areas of the Irish Republic. "Recruits are shown how to make up circuits and power units using putty in place of explosives but with real detonators. It scares the shit out of some of them. The putty is blown all over the place. You learn that once you have made a bomb you never touch it.

"You need to be a certain type of person and invariably you are an introvert, able to work on your own and not panic under pressure. You mustn't become stressed out - every move you make could cost not just your own life but that of every person in the street.

"Bomb-makers are a race apart, not because they are naturally like that but because you brood on what the devices do. I remember one chap telling me: 'It's so impersonal when the lads come to collect one. It's just a load of smelly bags and wire. Then when you see it on the news - devastation and death - you know you caused it but you feel nothing - that's hard to live with."

Donald likes a drink and loves to talk about the politics of Northern Ireland. He could recite details and dates of Republican 'spectaculars' [their most infamous atrocities] from memory. He claimed to have given up bomb-making but not necessarily for good. "The situation is ridiculous. The British Government could have done a deal with Sinn Fein [the IRA's political wing] but it back-pedalled. What else were they to do but end the cease-fire."

Donald accepted that he is an amateur, like all other 'volunteers', but he also saw himself as a soldier fighting a war against technically superior forces. He admitted that the British authorities were now constrained in the tactics they could use to defeat terrorism in Northern Ireland. But he was respectful of recent success by MI5, the internal security service, which has clearly obtained accurate intelligence about IRA active service units.

He predicted the Provisional IRA would split one day, with one small faction being formed that would employ much more deadly techniques. "About 1985, the INLA looked at the idea of spreading rabies around, but whereas the older volunteers were against using things like that, there are people now who are interested in chemi-

cal and biological devices.

"People are being taught about things like wind velocity using smoke bombs to test how gases might spread. I don't like it but these people are very committed."

ACROSS the world, bomb-makers use similar tactics to wreak devastation. In South Africa, the African National Congress under Nelson Mandela is now in power but it once fought a terrorist campaign against the racist apartheid regime using IRA-type tactics. What is interesting is how the Nationalist government responded. On the surface, it tried to convey an image of a responsible Western-style state. But the reality, details of which are now leaking out, was quite different: the Nationalist government secretly planned and executed appalling acts of brutality that amounted to nothing less than state terrorism.

The Truth and Reconciliation Commission, set up to give those involved a chance to confess in return for (in most cases) immunity from prosecution, has heard terrible stories of assassinations and a spate of dirty tricks operations designed to intimidate those fighting for racial equality and to frame the ANC. Even more illuminating has been the trial of Colonel Eugene De Kock, convicted to 212 years on 89 accounts including eight murders.

De Kock headed a secret police death squad called Vlakplaas (the name of a farm near Pretoria where the unit was based) which on one occasion murdered a man by bashing in his skull with a spade. Much of Vlakplaas's notorious past was exposed in 1989 by a former head, Captain Dirk Coetzee, who testified against De Kock. Coetzee's animosity to his colleague is understandable because at one time De Kock had also tried to kill him, as a warning to any other policemen who might be inclined to break ranks.

De Kock's plan was ingenious and lead to disaster as police 'technical man' and military intelligence agent, Steve Bosch, has disclosed. "After Coetzee's revelations about hit squad activities at Vlakplaas in 1989 everything at Vlakplaas was mixed up," Bosch said. "We destroyed some things and carted away weaponry because we thought they might come to inspect the farm.

"We had to find out where Coetzee was. We listened to his telephones, kept his house under observation and followed his family." Bosch said orders then came from De Kock to prepare a parcel for Coetzee. "I knew it had to be an explosive device because I couldn't prepare such a device on my own. I asked the technical section [of police security headquarters] for help."

Following orders from his commander, Bosch bought a 'Walkman' personal tape player and two music tapes. These were then sent to the security police's Rebecca Street branch in Pretoria where there was a printing press, and a mechanical and technical section. The mechanical section installed secret compartments in cars, built cameras into suitcases and the electronic engineers provided photographic and video equipment, and bugging devices. "Because I couldn't prepare such a device on my own, I asked the technical section for help," Bosch explained. After both Walkman's had been adapted, he was told to buy a sheep's head which he couldn't find. "Instead I bought a pig's head," Bosch explained. He said explosives had been placed in the earpieces of the headphones. The wire from the tape player set these off when the tape player was switched on. "We tried it on the pig's head and I told Col. De Kock it worked very well."

The court heard that in May 1990 the remaining cassette machine was put inside a padded-envelope marked "Evidence Hit Squads" with tapes of the singer Neil Diamond - Coetzee's favourite singer. It was then posted to an address to where Coetzee had been traced in Lusaka; but the plan went wrong. There was £10 excess postage on the parcel when it arrived and Coetzee did not pick it up. It was therefore returned to 'sender' and the name given on the packet was Bheki Mlangeni, a Johannesburg lawyer.

Tragically, Mlangeni - who was totally unaware that his name and address had been put on the pack - tried on the headphones and the device blew off his head. The South African intelligence services murdered the wrong man.

Much is written about how much South Africa has changed since those dark days but stories still circulate that the high-tech bomb-makers are still at work, producing weapons to order for customers around the world, including foreign governments. It seemed highly unlikely until a disturbing leaflet was handed to me in Johannesburg that advertises a "Sniper Event Recording System". It shows a sniper's rifle with a telescopic sight to which has been added a tiny video camera and a transmitter. The blurb begins: "This unique system will ensure positive identification and visual recording of hostile and illegal activities. High quality images can be transmitted to a command station or can be recorded on the spot. This recording system can be fitted on a sniper's standard telescope."

The horrific implication is that this device is intended for hired killers who need to provide their paymasters with proof they have done a 'good job'. We heard that the same laboratory was making briefcase bombs or booby traps from almost any common article. "They make the very best," said the informant, "and they are not very fussy about who they deal with."

Extract from a South African brochure describing how a hired killer can record a 'hit' on a victim or provide a live TV transmssion of the murder for his superiors.

SNIPER EVENT RECORDING SYSTEM

This unique system will ensure positive identification and permanent visual recording of hostile and illegal activities. High quality images can be transmitted to a command station or can be recorded on the spot. This recording system can be fitted on a sniper's standard telescope . This system may also be used for effective training of riflemen. Standard video equipment can be used. Equipment used on the system will depend on the quality and requirements specified.

Chapter Two

A TROUBLED PROVINCE

The Provisional Irish Republican Army, known widely as the IRA, is one of the more dangerous and professional terrorist groups in the world. During the last two decades the activities of this organisation with their ability to strike anywhere and against almost any target have confounded the authorities and security services. The IRA has also inspired other groups to adopt its tactics. Its modus operandi and its motives must therefore be understood if the future threat posed by terrorism is to be fully appreciated.

Ireland has seen extraordinary violence and 300 years of division, but what are the roots of the conflict? The basic causes of the current problems are partition and religion. Partition dates back to the English King James I (1566-1625) who settled English and Scots in the province called Ulster in the northern part of the island. The Protestantism of the settlers clashed with the Catholicism of the native Irish, and moreover, the settlers took the best land. The few indigenous Irish who actually kept their holdings had to pay high rents and had no security of tenure. It all led to rebellion.

In 1642 a massacre was followed by the conquest of Ireland by Oliver Cromwell and another period of terror. The struggle between William III, of Orange, and James II of England, was fought out in Ireland. On 12th July 1690 William won at the battle of the Boyne, which is still energetically commemorated today by the Protestants of Northern Ireland (mainly the Orange Order, whose influence in the North is overwhelming), and a new period of Protestant ascendancy began. Catholics could hold no office or possess land in their own country or trade in competition with English merchants. These harsh restrictions were only relaxed somewhat in 1750.

A crucial event in Irish history was the Act of Union of 1800, which made Ireland part of the Union stripped of the power to legislate for itself. Since 1800 an element in Ireland has always been

dedicated to overthrowing the Act by armed force. This element evolved into the Irish Republican Brotherhood and then to the IRA and Provisional IRA (PIRA).

The centuries of rebellion and violent repression with Protestant fighting Catholic have given Irish conflicts, including IRA activities, a strong religious element. The divide between Protestant Unionists and Catholics in Northern Ireland is truly ethnic. The Catholics regard themselves as Irish in every sense whereas the Protestants think of themselves as British with little Irish identity.

The Democratic Unionist Party and the more moderate Ulster Unionist party, led by David Trimble, believe that the survival of the Protestant identity in the North is at stake. They say that if the Republicans win and the North is united with Eire, the Protestants will be a minority of 1 million in a state with 3.3 million Catholics.

In a united Ireland, the Protestants would be subject to the Republic's laws on divorce and abortion and to the Republic's education system, all of which they find objectionable. But above all else, the Protestants in the North fear the loss of their right to British citizenship.

It must not be forgotten that because of this troubled background there are two major terrorist traditions in Northern Ireland: Republican and Loyalist (those wanting Northern Ireland to remain part of the United Kingdom). In the early 1970s, according to official

A demonstration of strength by members of the Ulster Freedom Fighters, a pro-British paramilitary organisation in Northern Ireland

figures, Northern Ireland Protestants owned about 107,000 licensed weapons. The Ulster Volunteer Force (UVF) - which was originally formed in 1912 with British support to oppose Home Rule for Ireland - and the Ulster Defence Association (UDA), are paramilitary

Loyalist forces set up to defend Unionism and to fight the IRA. And like the IRA they are both outlawed.

The Research Institute for the Study of Conflict and Terrorism (RISCT), estimates that between 1970 and 1994 (when the IRA declared a temporary cease-fire), about 3,000 of the 1.5 million strong population of Northern Ireland were killed through the conflict and more than 30,000 were injured. Of these deaths, about 1,500 have been in violence between British forces and the IRA; approximately 1,700 deaths were caused by other paramilitary organisations such as the Ulster Volunteer Force and the Ulster Freedom Fighters. The cost of the violence during this 24-year period was, according to the Bank of Ireland, nearly £500 million each year.

The beginning of this carnage can be traced back to 1969 when there was increasing civil disturbance in Northern Ireland in protest at discrimination against the Catholic minority. On August 14, 1969, Harold Wilson, the British Prime Minister, ordered large numbers of British soldiers to be sent there.

There was rioting on the streets, yet the IRA did little to defend the Catholics in the North. It is said that only about six IRA men

---

After the IRA split in 1970, the Official IRA was quickly overshadowed by the success of the armed struggle conducted by the PIRA. After two years, the Official IRA declared a truce and then an indefinite cease-fire. Those who remain active continue to work for the unification of the 32 counties by political means, and their aim is to unite Protestant and Catholic workers into an Irish Socialist republic.

But in 1974, the Official IRA split again. A militant Marxist group decided to pursue a violent revolutionary struggle against the British and formed the Irish Republican Socialist Party (IRSP). Within a few months, a paramilitary wing of the IRSP emerged, calling itself INLA. While the group has remained much smaller than the PIRA - it is estimated that the INLA has no more than 50 active members - its operations can be much more ruthless and violent.

Yet another splinter group emerged in 1987: the Irish People's Liberation Organisation (IPLO). There has been much bitter fighting and feuding among the members of the Official IRA, the INLA, and the IPLO. Although neither of the two groups have the strength to mount large-scale operations, they have launched occasional bloody attacks, and certainly should not be ignored. For example, the INLA murdered the British Member of Parliament, Airey Neave, by blowing up his car as he drove out of the House of Commons car park, using a bomb with a mercury switch triggering device.

took to the streets of Belfast during the rioting. However, if this hand-ful had not been there, mobs led by B-Specials (an armed special constabulary drawn from Protestant paramilitary groups) would have burned the Falls Road, a mainly Catholic area of Belfast.

Whether to take direct action or seek a political solution was fiercely debated within the IRA and in 1970 it split, between the more dovish Official IRA and the Provisionals, who wanted a military solu-tion. The Provisional IRA concentrated its activities in Northern Ireland at first, orchestrating a campaign of violence. The aim was not to gain an absolute military victory over the British forces in the North, which numbered some 18,000 troops. The plan was to destabilise the state and make it ungovernable so that British mili-tary forces would be forced to withdraw.

THE STRATEGY of the Provisional IRA is described in its so-called Green Book and it forms a blueprint for many other terrorist groups. It calls for: "a war of attrition against enemy personnel which is aimed at causing as many casualties and deaths as possible so as to create a demand from their people at home for their withdrawal. A bombing campaign aimed at making the enemy's financial interest in our country unprofitable while at the same time curbing long term financial investment in our country. To make the Six Counties as at present and for the past several years ungovernable except by colo-nial military rule. To sustain the war and gain support for its ends by national and international propaganda and publicity campaigns. By defending the war of liberation by punishing criminals, collaborators and informers."

Support for PIRA was greatly boosted by the British govern-ment's decision, on August 9, 1971, to opt for internment without trial: Catholics, but no Protestants, were seized and locked up. Most of them had little to do with the IRA or were completely innocent yet they were badly treated. Support was further boosted by the Bloody Sunday massacre of January 30, 1972, when the British Parachute Regiment opened fire on an unarmed civil rights demon-

stration in Londonderry, killing 14 people. Outrage about the massacre was increased considerably when the official inquiry, by Lord Widgery, attached no blame to the paratroopers. The Catholics understandably regarded the inquiry as a whitewash, and that period after publication of the Widgery report was probably the time of greatest popular support for the republican army.

In 1970 the PIRA detonated about 170 bombs inside or outside public houses or in cars, almost all of them in Belfast. But the number of shootings and bombings increased dramatically in 1971 and 1972. In 1971, there were 1,756 shootings; in 1972 there were a staggering 10,628. In 1971 1,515 explosive devices were used, compared with 1,853 in 1972.

More people were killed (467) and injured in Northern Ireland in 1972 than in any other year since 1969 and clearly something had to be done. On March 24, 1972, the Northern Ireland government at Stormont in Belfast was suspended, since when Northern Ireland has been ruled directly from Westminster. However, the violence escalated - it was reported that in February 1978 napalm was used to destroy the La Mon restaurant in Belfast - and the British Royal Family became a target.

Terrorists embarked on an ambitious plot to assassinate the Queen. A special bomb, fitted with a mechanism to delay the detonation, exploded a few hours after the Queen visited Coleraine University in Co. Derry. On August 27, 1979, Earl Mountbatten and his grandson were killed when his boat was blown up at Mullaghmore, Co. Sligo. Mountbatten had spent every August there for 30 years, always without a bodyguard.

When the 'Troubles' began in the early 70s, the PIRA had few weapons stockpiled but, financed by bank robberies and donations, it rapidly remedied that problem by buying from the international arms black-market, and from other terrorist groups, as a few arms seizures by the authorities showed.

On October 17, 1971 the Dutch police captured a large haul of Czech-made weapons at Schipol Airport, Amsterdam, including bazookas, rocket-launchers, hand grenades, machine guns and

rifles. There were enough weapons to fill 166 crates. Another large consignment was seized on March 28, 1973 by the Irish Republic's security services on board the Claudia, a 298-ton motor vessel registered in Cyprus. The haul included 250 rifles, 240 small arms, anti-tank mines and explosives. On July 4, 1975 Canadian police captured a variety of weapons in raids in Toronto, St Catherines, Tavistock, and Windsor, Ontario, including machine guns, Sten guns, semi-automatic weapons, hand grenades, and ammunition.

On December 21, 1977, Dublin police captured a shipment of arms in Antwerp on board the Tower Stream. The arms, supplied by the Palestinian Liberation Organisation, included two Bren guns, 29 Kalashnikov rifles, 29 sub-machine guns, more than 100 hand grenades, thousands of rounds of ammunition of various kinds, rocket-launchers and rockets, and large amounts of TNT and plastic explosives.

In Northern Ireland itself virtually all types of small arms have been found, as well as rocket-propelled grenades, hand grenades, semi-automatic rifles, sub-machine guns and machine guns, Kalashnikov and Armalite rifles, heavier weapons, and so on. In November 1987, 150 tonnes of weapons were seized off the coast of France, on board a boat called the Eksund. It turned out that at least four other shipments had successfully reached Eire before the Eksund was stopped. Intensive searches were mounted throughout Eire but only a small number of arms were found.

THE PIRA was originally based on a military-style structure with brigades, battalions and companies. However, because the security services were able to infiltrate these units, the PIRA leadership changed in the late 1970s to a cell-type structure. The cells, called Active Service Units (ASUs), each contain between five and eight members but sometimes more (perhaps up to 12 members), for terrorist operations, and the number in a particular cell is often chosen according to the requirements of a particular operation.

Each cell operates independently, with its own arsenal of

weapons and explosives and is responsible for obtaining its own intelligence. There are probably eleven or twelve ASUs operating around Northern Ireland. Because members of one cell do not know the identities of members of other cells, it has proved difficult for the security services to infiltrate them. According to Jane's Intelligence Review estimates, there are some 100 active PIRA members in the Belfast area, about 80 in Londonderry, and 40 or so in South Armagh. About a third (80) of these hard-core members comprise the key members of the ASUs. The remaining 140 or so PIRA members assist the hard-core people in the ASUs - the foot-soldiers or Volunteers as they are called - as and when required. Once experienced, the foot-soldiers may be promoted to hard-core members when the latter are promoted to senior roles in the organisation.

In addition to these fighting members, there are active supporters of the PIRA (called 'Auxiliaries') who are prepared to perform subsidiary tasks for the ASUs: delivering weapons, driving vehicles, watching out for the security forces, and so on. There are also a large number of people in the general population who sympathise with the PIRA, providing a pool of potential recruits, fund-raisers, and safe houses. The number of people in Northern Ireland who fully support the methods and actions of the PIRA can only be guessed at, but it is probably roughly 20,000 or 30,000.

It appears that there are plenty of recruits to the PIRA in the North and South of Ireland. However it should be remembered that some terrorist attacks in Northern Ireland have particularly outraged Catholics, losing the PIRA much sympathy and support. In July 1990, for example, a young nun was killed by a PIRA bomb. Tactics took a new turn on October 24, 1990 when three ordinary Catholic civilians described by the PIRA as "collaborators", were forced to drive bombs to military installations, where they were detonated without putting PIRA people at risk. The use of human bombs was intended to intimidate those serving or supplying the security forces and to deter other civilians from aiding the security forces. In November 1991 the PIRA bombed a hospital in Belfast,

killing two soldiers and injuring a number of children in the children's ward. Yet PIRA members are highly professional terrorists and they learn by their mistakes. In the words of RISCT: "One should not underestimate the intensity of the PIRA's efforts constantly to improve the training and expertise of their operations. One only has to study the 'Green Book' and the track record of the organisation to recognise the emphasis given to the acquisition of basic terrorist skills, such as intelligence gathering, weaponry, internal security, use of safe houses, false documents, acquisition of vehicles for terrorist operations and so on......the PIRA are striving to obtain more sophisticated technological expertise by giving their members advanced training in such fields as electronics and telecommunications."

WITHOUT DOUBT the PIRA is one of the best armed terrorist groups in the world today. An astonishing array of weapons have been accumulated during their campaign. The publication 'Jane's Intelligence Review' estimates the PIRA has an arsenal of 60 Webley 0.455 revolvers, 650 AK-47 assault rifles, a few dozen Armalite assault rifles, one Barrett M82A1 sniper rifle, 12 7.62 mm FN machine guns, 20 12.7x107 mm DshK heavy machine guns, 40 RPG-7 rocket launchers (this Soviet weapon can penetrate up to 320 mm of armour), one SAM7 surface-to-air missile, and 6 LPO-50 flame throwers.

In addition, it is though to have stockpiled about 3 tonnes of Semtex explosive and about 600 detonators for bombs. This amount of Semtex is enough to make hundreds of devices - 10 kilograms will produce a large explosion. It is also used as a primary charge for fertiliser bombs, for which unlimited supplies of chemicals can be easily bought.

Even if they return to the level of violence in the 1970s and 1980s, the current PIRA arsenal will keep it going for at least another decade, and it is rich enough to buy many more weapons. How serviceable their stockpiles are, however, is not known; their SAM-7 surface-to-air missile, for example, may not actually work.

The PIRA has obtained these weapons from many sources, mainly the USA, but also including the former Soviet Union, Eastern Europe, Arab countries, and other terrorist groups. The generosity of Libya's Colonel Ghadaffi in supplying arms and explosives to the PIRA has been well publicised. It is reported that in the mid-1980s, Libya despatched about 1,000 Armalite and AK47 assault rifles, a number of heavy machine guns, 12 SAM-7 surface-to-air missiles, and more than a tonne of Semtex explosive.

Libya now claims it has stopped supplying weapons to the PIRA but it was a crucial source for many years. John Barron, in his authoritative book, 'The Secret Work of Society Secret Agents' named other countries: "The KGB has worked secretly through Czech, Cuban, and Arab terrorist intermediaries to arm and train both wings of the IRA. The Cuban operational plan for 1972 drafted under KGB supervision stipulated that the Cubans would train Irish Republican Army personnel in the tactics of terrorism and guerrilla war."

DURING THE 1930s, those IRA members who favoured violence, 'the bullet and the bomb', rather than political means to achieve a United Ireland, came to the conclusion that the war with the British should be carried onto the mainland. However before 1970 the IRA was simply too weak militarily to conduct such operations. Nevertheless, an ill-conceived bombing campaign, carried out by a small, perhaps twelve-strong, group of IRA men began in England on January 12, 1939. It lasted about a year and a half. Bombs were let off in London, the Midlands and the North. The worst incident was an explosion on August 25, 1939 in Coventry which killed 12 people and injured 52.

A new bombing campaign began on the mainland on March 8, 1972 with explosions at the Old Bailey court and Whitehall, the heart of the British government. Apart from some periods of relatively little violent activity, the campaign has gone on ever since, with a 17-month temporary cease-fire between August 1994 and February 1996.

Forensic scientists search through the debris following the M62 coach bombing in which ten adults and two children were murdered.

Mainland attacks have been devastating. In February 1974 a coach was blown up on the M62 motorway killing nine soldiers and three civilians, two of them children. In October 1974 bombs in public houses in Guildford and Woolwich killed a total of seven people. Then on November 21, 1974, two public houses in Birmingham were devastated by explosions which killed 21 people and injured 168. A number of shootings and bombings in London in 1974 - including a bomb in the Tower of London - and 1975 severely disrupted social and commercial life in the capital.

There was a lull until late 1978 when the campaign on the mainland started again. The violent events which took place are too numerous to describe in detail. But some were particularly horrific. On July 20, 1982, for example, two bombs exploded in London. One went off in Hyde Park killing four soldiers from the Household Cavalry and the other exploded in Regent's Park killing seven Royal Greenjackets bandsmen.

The Hyde Park bomb contained about 12 kilograms of nails. As well as killing the Cavalrymen a number of horses died; the combination seemed to incense the public in both Britain and Ireland. Funds were raised in Eire to 'compensate' the families of the dead soldiers and replace the horses. Then, just before Christmas 1983, a car bomb exploded outside Harrod's department store in Kensington, killing six people and injuring 90, some seriously.

As shown in Chapter One, the PIRA developed great skills in designing and fabricating bombs: fuses with long and very precise time delays and complex radio-controlled devices have been their speciality. A long time delay mechanism was used in the bomb which exploded in the Grand Hotel, Brighton, on October 12, 1984 at which Prime Minister Margaret Thatcher and members of her Cabinet were staying during a Conservative Party Conference. The blast killed five people and injured many more.

It was a nightmarish spectacle. The sight of the carnage on television, showing how close the PIRA came to eliminating the Prime Minister, who very narrowly escaped death, and the entire British Cabinet came as a great shock to the British people, particularly because the bombing happened in spite of the huge amount of security surrounding the conference.

The day in 1984 when the IRA tried to blow up the entire British Cabinet. An advanced time-bomb was detonated above a bedroom occupied by the Prime Minister, Margaret Thatcher. She survived but five people were killed.

And so it went on. In 1989 a bomb attack on a Marine barracks in Deal, Kent killed 11 Marine bandsmen and wounded 20. In 1990, Ian Gow, a pro-Unionist Conservative MP was

blown up by a bomb put under his car.

In 1991, targets attacked included the prestigious Carlton Club, Piccadilly, ordinary railway stations, and main line stations in London. The attacks on railway stations were particularly disruptive, and were exacerbated by hoax calls which often stopped the entire London Underground during rush hour. On April 10, 1992, the Baltic Exchange building in St Mary Axe in the heart of the City of London was gutted by a large bomb containing 45 kilograms of Semtex in a Transit van, killing three people and injuring about 91. The economic cost of the bombing was estimated at up to £1 billion. On the same day, another bomb in a Transit van exploded on the A-5 flyover at Staples Corner, North London. The explosion caused huge traffic jams, disrupting life in Northwest London.

A year later, in April 1993, the City of London was attacked again when a large bomb exploded at Bishopsgate, killing a newspaper photographer. The total damage to the City may well exceed £2 billion. On the day of the Bishopsgate attack, bombs exploded at Finsbury Park and King's Cross in taxis hijacked by the PIRA. Then, in March 1993, came an attack which sickened the world: a bomb in a shopping centre in Warrington, Cheshire, killed two small boys and caused an outcry in Britain and Ireland. But still the campaign continued: three huge bombs were intercepted in England before detonation in 1992 and 1994. A van bomb was found outside Britain's tallest office block in Canary Wharf and another was discovered in North London. The latter was in a box van and contained as much as about three tonnes of explosive. The third was discovered in July 1994 in a lorry at the port of Heysham, Lancashire.

On February 7, 1991 the PIRA made their most daring attack on the mainland. Prime Minister John Major was sitting in the Cabinet Room in 10 Downing Street with a number of Cabinet Ministers discussing the progress of the Gulf War, when a PIRA rocket exploded in the garden of Number 10. The rocket was one of three fired from a mortar manufactured by the PIRA. The mortar was carried in a van and the rockets were fired through holes cut in its roof. The van was parked about a hundred metres from the back of 10

Downing Street and, incredible though it may seem, the whole exercise took place in broad daylight.

The police guarding the area around Downing Street should have known the PIRA had access to mortars, because they had used other multi-barrelled mortars carried on trucks or vans. For example, on February 28, 1985, the Royal Ulster Constabulary barracks at Newry Co. Down was attacked with mortars made from steel tubes, about 1.4 metres in length and fixed to the floor of a stolen lorry. The mortars, fired at a range of about 200 metres, destroyed a canteen, killing nine RUC officers and injuring 32 more.

The PIRA have considerably improved the accuracy and reliability of these improvised weapons. The most recent design is the so-called Mark-17 mortar, developed in 1995 during the cease-fire, and

A police officer in front of a burning van from which three mortars were fired at the British Prime Minister's residence in central London

tested in the Carlingford Lough area, south of the border. The new mortar is described as the most destructive weapon in the PIRA's current arsenal.

The design and construction of these weapons demonstrate the technical sophistication of the PIRA. Another weapon it developed is a hollow-charge cylindrical grenade containing Semtex called a 'drogue'. When the pin of the grenade is removed, a device is released which makes the grenade strike its target at such an angle that the hollow charge has the maximum destructive effect on the target. When used properly, the drogue grenade can be an effective

weapon against the armoured troop carriers and Land Rovers used by the security forces in Northern Ireland.

SINCE THE 1970s the terrorist war was also being waged against British targets on the Continent, particularly the military. In the Netherlands the British Ambassador was murdered and seven bandsmen and a number of civilians were injured in 1979 when a British Military Band was attacked with a bomb.

The scale of the violence abroad is surprising: between 1987 and 1990, British soldiers were attacked with guns and bombs on the Continent on about two dozen occasions.

Early in 1988, the PIRA decided to expand its activities to Gibraltar. The plan was to attack a British 'changing of the guard' ceremony using a bomb in a car. Two men and a woman were sent to carry out the bombing. Before going to Gibraltar the three terrorists checked into a hotel in Spain. The Spanish authorities discovered their passports were false and informed the British, through Interpol.

They were kept under close surveillance and then the British government decided to send an SAS special-forces team to Gibraltar to prevent the bombing. On March 6, the three PIRA terrorists who had parked a car in the centre of Gibraltar were shot dead by the SAS squad. The car was found to contain no explosives but later another vehicle was found in Spain with a bomb and detonators in its boot.

The incident aroused huge controversy in the Catholic community with the British government accused of deliberately executing the PIRA members. But on May 1, 1988 three Royal Air Force men were killed in separate attacks in the Netherlands, while in Germany the following year the tiny daughter of one British soldier and the wife of another were killed. In May 1990 two Australian tourists were killed in the Netherlands after PIRA gunmen apparently mistook them for off-duty British soldiers. These incidents outraged almost all Irish people, losing the PIRA much sympathy and support.

IN 1994 a section of PIRA appears to have been persuaded they could not achieve a united Ireland purely by military means and that some sort of political solution should be attempted through negotiations between political parties in the North - Republican and Unionist - and the London and Dublin governments. A PIRA cease-fire was called on 31st August 1994; it was followed in October 1994 by a cease-fire called by Loyalist paramilitaries. Sadly, discussions between the parties took so long that hard-liners in the PIRA re-asserted their dominance and the cease-

Destruction of an office block at Broadgate in the City of London during the height of the IRA's bombing campaign.

fire was broken on February 9, 1996 when a huge bomb devastated the Canary Wharf business district in London.

A trailer lorry packed with explosives was detonated outside a high-rise building, killing two newsagents and causing millions of pounds worth of damage. A number of other bombs followed: on February 15, a small bomb exploded in a telephone box in Charing Cross Road, London. On February 18, a PIRA man, Edward O'Brien, was killed when the bomb he was transporting exploded accidentally on a London Transport bus in the Aldwych, London. On March 9, a small bomb went off in the Old Brompton Road, Fulham followed by another on April 17, in an empty house in Earl's Court, London. On April 24, two large bombs, containing the largest amount of

Semtex ever found on the mainland, failed to detonate on Hammersmith Bridge, a busy commuter route over the River Thames.

On June 17, there was a major blast in the centre of Manchester. The bomb, one of the most powerful ever exploded on the mainland, used roughly one and a half tonnes of explosive based on fertiliser, primed with Semtex. It was carried on a 7.5 tonnes Ford Cargo truck and exploded between the Arndale shopping centre and a Marks & Spencers store.

The explosion produced a crater under the van approximately 10 meters in diameter and caused damage over one square mile of the city centre. Tens of thousands of people were in the area on the day but, miraculously, no-one was killed, although 206 people were

Three IRA bombs destroyed the Tern Hill barracks, home of Britain's Parachute Regiment in February 1989 creating a large crater.

injured, mainly by flying glass. The economic cost of the blast was put at £300m. More than 400 businesses were affected by the explosion, which severely damaged the commercial heart of Manchester.

The Quebec British army barracks in Osnabruck, Germany, became a target on June 28. Three mortars were fired from a Ford Transit flat-bed truck near the main gate. The mortar tubes were screwed to the floor of truck and covered with tarpaulins. The mortars were fired by a timer device in the cab. The mortar shells were made from gas bottles, each packed with 80 kilograms of home-made explosive and provided with a 2.2 kilogram booster charge. The target was apparently two fuel pumps on the base but only one of the shells exploded and this one missed the target.

Events in 1996 therefore showed the PIRA was still a highly effective terrorist force, with the technology and expertise to be reckoned with, and with the capability to fabricate munitions from readily obtainable components. It also still had access to large sums of money.

The cost of administering the organisation is considerable; as well as financing a war, there is the need to provide hundreds of jailed PIRA terrorists and their families with financial assistance. Businesses, legal and illegal, are operated so that profits can go to the PIRA, but these businesses also require substantial initial investment. Last but not least, PIRA activities in Northern Ireland and on the Continent have to be paid for, and the members on operations have to be supported. Where does such an illegal organisation acquire all this money?

The RISCT answers the question by quoting estimates given, in about 1990, by the Northern Ireland Office. According to the Office's figures, the PIRA then had an annual income of £5.3 million. Tax fraud accounted for about £1 million; legitimate business made about £1 million; and public houses, drinking clubs and gaming machines brought in another £1 million. Protection rackets and extortion accounted for £500,000 and the sale of pirate videos and smuggling for another £600,000. Donations from supporters in the USA and other countries provided £100,000.

THE PIRA is involved in a number of criminal rackets, such as trading in illegal tapes and pornographic films and there is also compelling evidence of PIRA involvement in the illegal drugs trade, at the same time as claiming it is strongly opposed to drugs (it regularly punishes civilians it claims are drug-pushers). Robberies,

extortion, and protection money, particularly from small businesses, help to swell the coffers. A mark of the conflict in Northern Ireland is the fact that the police appear to be almost wholly ineffective in preventing this type of organised crime.

Chapter Three

TOOLS OF THE TRADE

Terrorists are becoming increasingly sophisticated in their choice of weaponry, but their arsenal's are still largely comprised of bombs and bullets. As the IRA has demonstrated, the list is long and includes guns (pistols, revolvers, rifles, assault rifles, sub-machine guns, and light and heavy machine guns), hand-held missile launchers, bombs, mines, and improvised mortars and grenades.

The weapon most favoured is perhaps the Kalashnikov AK47 assault rifle. Sub-machine guns are also extremely popular with terrorists. There are more than 150 models available and they can be obtained world-wide, often by mail order with no questions asked. Top of the range assault rifles and sub-machine guns can be bought for less than $1,000 each. Pump-action and automatic shot guns are also readily available. They are lethal at ranges of up to 30 metres but they are not easy to conceal.

Some terrorist groups use rocket propelled grenades, particularly the Russian RPG7, against buildings and vehicles including armoured vehicles. These unguided missiles are not very effective except at short range. Guided missiles are considerably more effective. They are, however, normally too expensive for most terrorist groups although some have used them. The US Milan and

A Tejas 50-calibre sniper's rifle used by the IRA in single shot killings of security force members.

Russian AT4 are the anti-tank missiles of choice. They are very effective against, for example, an armoured limousine, and can cover a range of two kilometres in about 12 seconds. The missile and its launcher can be carried in the boot of a car.

Surface-to-air missiles (SAMs) have been used by sub-national groups to shoot down civil and military aircraft, including helicopters. The Americans supplied a large number of Stinger SAMs to the Mujahedin rebels in Afghanistan who used them effectively against Soviet helicopters.

SAMs are traded on the black-market and are therefore available to those terrorist groups with enough cash. The missile contains its own guidance system so that, once fired, it seeks out and attacks the target without further instructions from an operator. The guidance system may use radar or a heat-seeking device.

Some terrorist groups have shown that they can make their own multiple mortars, grenades, and land mines. Mortars and mines can be fired by remote control, using, for example, an electronic signal. Some home-made devices designed and manufactured by terrorists have become very sophisticated.

BOMBS are still the main weapon in the terrorist's arsenal because their use frequently kills and injures many people and their blasts cause great destruction accounting for considerable economic loss. They are also a powerful psychological weapon which can cow entire communities.

The number of bomb attacks in recent decades is quite astonishing. If we take Northern Ireland as an example, we find that in 26 years of operation, the Provisional IRA have used about 14,000 explosive devices. The cost of the destruction caused by just four of these bombs on the mainland of Britain - three that exploded in 1992, 1993 and 1996 in London and one in 1996 in Manchester - is estimated to amount to about £1,000,000,000.

The use of bombs is increasing because the necessary technical information to make them is readily available on the Internet and in public libraries. In America, the number of people using bombs to attack other members of the public has nearly doubled this decade. Oliver Revell, the former head of criminal investigations for the FBI, has been quoted as saying: "There is a lot of hostility and anger pent-up in our society. And the bomb is a cheap and easy, and sometimes a very difficult-to-solve way, of carrying out retribution, assassination and murder. It has become a tool of preference."

Official statistics supplied by the Bureau of Alcohol, Tobacco and Firearms (ATF) in the US show that 1,699 bombings were either attempted or actually happened across America in 1989. In 1994, just five years later (and the last year for which full figures are available), that figure had increased to 3,163 incidents. According to Richard A. Rawlins, the deputy associate director of the ATF: "The materials for making bombs have about the same availability [as several years ago], but it's just the information became more readily available to a number of criminals."

One recent case in Baton Rouge, Louisiana, illustrates the difficulties facing the American authorities. An 18-year-old allegedly persuaded two friends to help her murder her parents to get their life insurance money. The young woman and her accomplices read bomb-making instructions they found on the Internet, stole the materials necessary to make a bomb from several high school chemistry laboratories, and then plotted to blow-up a train bringing the woman's parents home from a holiday.

The woman and her friends were not among the brightest students - all three were college drop-outs - but they were still able to put a murderous plan into operation. It was only foiled at the last minute. Other attempts by members of the public to use explosives have been more successful. In New York, a man sent six letter-bombs to relatives of his girlfriend; five people were killed when four exploded.

THE WORLD may becoming acculturated to bombings and violent death and anyone studying events in the Middle East in the last

twenty years would understand why that may be the case. In this period, Lebanon was a cockpit of terrorism, perpetrated on national, international, and state levels. Violence of one sort or another completely destroyed the quality of life in Beirut, making what was once a beautiful city into the most dangerous place on earth.

Earlier in 1983, on the April 18, a bomb at the US Embassy in Beirut. A truck carrying a large amount of explosive was detonated, killing 63 people, 17 of them American, and injuring 100. The CIA section in the region was virtually eliminated in the attack. Then on October 23, came two more atrocities.

A truck driven at great speed by a suicide bomber bulldozed past the sentry post into the compound of the American Marines, a four-storey concrete building. The bomb was a complex device boosted by an explosive gas which detonated with a power equivalent to that of 5.4 tonnes of TNT, killing 241 Marines. It is remembered as one of the world's worst ever terrorist attacks, and the most powerful ever terrorist explosion. Within a few seconds of the explosion at the US Marine Barracks, a second suicide bomber attacked the French army battalion, killing 59 soldiers.

The American and French troops were part of the Multi-National Force (MNF) sent to Beirut after Christian Phalangist Lebanese troops massacred about 2,000 Palestinians over a two-day period at the two Palestinian refugee camps, Sabra and Chatila, in September 1982. The world had found it easy to ignore much of the brutality and massacres executed by the various fighting factions in Lebanon. But Sabra and Chatila were different because the Israeli army was involved. Not only had they asked the Phalangists to go into the camps, ostensibly to kill any Palestinian Liberation Organisation fighters remaining there, but they allegedly stood by at the edge of the camps while the killings and atrocities went on.

The Israelis had invaded Lebanon on June 6, 1982 with the specific objective of eliminating the PLO to prevent further attacks on Israel. By the time they withdrew at the end of 1983 it is estimated about 18,000 people were killed and some 30,000 wounded, the vast majority being Palestinian or Lebanese civilians. It must have been hard for the citizens of Beirut to distinguish between the terrorism of the PLO and the violence and horror of the Israeli attack. For them, the Israelis use of such vicious weapons as phosphorous bombs, which caused terrible injuries and agonising slow death and which left bodies, including children's, burning for hours, was terrorism.

The MNF, made up of American, French, and Italian troops, was sent to the Lebanon to prevent new massacres by the Christian Phalangists, or anyone else, and to re-establish the authority of the Lebanese government (ironically a Christian Phalangist government) in the aftermath of the Israeli invasion. But the descent of Lebanon into chaos showed no sign of stopping. On September 14, 1982, Bashir Gemayel, the newly elected Lebanese President, was assassinated by a large bomb which blew up his party's Beirut offices. Could the MFN restore a semblance of stability?

A new terrorist group, Islamic Jihad (Islamic Holy War) also known as Hezbollah, made sure it did not. In March 1983 the group launched a series of attacks on MNF troops and the terrible slaughter that April and October was also its doing. Within six months the MNF was out of Beirut and Islamic Jihad's terrorist campaign had succeeded.

Jihad, which probably has a strength of several thousand, is a radical Shi'a group formed in the Lebanon and working for the creation of an Islamic republic (similar to the one in Iran) in Lebanon. The group reportedly receives money, training, weapons, explosives, and other aid from Iran and it has been responsible for many anti-US terrorist attacks apart from the bombing of the US Marine Barracks in Beirut. Islamic Jihad has also made many attacks on Israel including attacks from South Lebanon using Katusha multi-rocket launchers.

THE IRANIAN connection may also explain recent bombings of American installations by Islamic Fundamentalists in Saudi Arabia. On June 26, 1996 a large bomb containing about 1.3 tonnes of explo-

sive and carried in a 5,000-gallon diesel fuel truck, exploded at the perimeter of the King Abdul-Aziz air base at Dhahran, in the eastern province of Saudi Arabia.

A large contingent of American servicemen are stationed at the base, along with smaller contingents from France and Britain. The explosion left a crater about 10 metres deep and went off 30 metres from an apartment block housing families. The eight-storey building was devastated, 19 American servicemen were killed, and another 80 people were seriously wounded.

An unknown group, the Legion of the Martyr Abdullah al-Huzaifi, claimed responsibility for the attack, which may have been in revenge for the public beheading of four terrorists found guilty of the car bombing of the American-run Saudi national Guard training centre in Riyadh in November 1995. That bombing had been carried out by Islamic Fundamentalists (two previously unknown Islamic groups, the Tigers of the Gulf and the Movement for Islamic Change claimed responsibility) and five Americans and two Indians were killed.

The Lockerbie disaster was the third bombing of commercial airliners in three and a half years. The other atrocities were the blowing up of an Air India flight over the Atlantic Ocean in 1985, which killed 329, and the destruction of the Korean Airlines flight over Burma in 1987 in which 115 died..

THIS STORY of carnage in the Middle East, and the hatred unleashed at the major Western powers, particularly the USA, has many repercussions. Until Wednesday December 21, 1988, few had ever heard of the small town in Scotland called Lockerbie but at three minutes past seven that evening a bomb in the forward cargo section of Pan American Flight 103 (The Maid of the Seas) exploded high in the air above.

The Boeing 747 Jumbo Jet had begun its journey in Frankfurt, first flying to London's Heathrow airport before beginning the flight from Heathrow towards New York's Kennedy airport. It was at an altitude of 9,500 metres when it was completely destroyed by the blast, probably by someone with a Middle East link.*

There have been many ramifications to the downing of Flight-103. A number of Western intelligence agencies are probably embroiled in some way and, for their own reasons, many authorities

appear to be unwilling to co-operate fully with the police investigations. The investigations were also muddied by the anti-Libyan polices of the British and the American governments. The details and the evolution of events surrounding it are therefore of considerable importance to those interested in studying terrorism and political violence.

Two hundred and seventy people were killed in this, Britain's worst ever air disaster. The dead included 243 passengers and 16 crew as well as 11 Lockerbie residents killed when the debris from the downed aircraft hit the ground. Who blew up Flight 103? How was it done? What was the motive for the outrage? No-one still really knows other than those who committed this horrendous act.

There are two theories about the perpetrators: one blames the Popular Front for the Liberation of Palestine General Command for the bombing. However this is rejected by the British and American governments who blame Libya. British Prime Minister John Major, for example, on June 6, 1996 (after calling the investigation into the bombing "the most intensive investigation in United Kingdom history") said the possible involvement of a Palestinian terrorist group was explored during the early stages of the investigation. He added: "No credible evidence emerged to substantiate its involvement in the Lockerbie crime. It is for a jury to decide how reliable the evidence is, but successive Lord Advocates would not have brought and maintained charges if they had believed that the evidence on which they were based was unreliable, incomplete or fabricated."

The charges brought by Scotland's Lord Advocate, referred to by the Prime Minister, were against two Libyans named as planting the device. The American Grand Jury in the District Court of Columbia also charged two Libyan citizens with sabotaging PanAm 103. They were officers of the Libyan Intelligence Services who worked for Libyan Airlines.

Tam Dayell, the Scottish Labour Member of Parliament for Linlithgow, a persistent campaigner to get justice done for the victims of Lockerbie, believes that British Ministers are ignoring important new evidence which casts serious doubt on the allega-

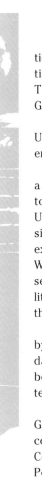

tion the two Libyans are guilty. He argues the Scottish legal authorities were pressurised by former British Prime Minister Margaret Thatcher and former American Presidents Ronald Reagan and George Bush into suppressing the truth.

It is said they used the bombing to justify the imposition of United Nations sanctions against Libya, a regime these political leaders detested.

Why should they do so? When in office, ex-President Reagan had a fixation about Colonel Ghadaffi, the Libyan leader, declaring Libya to be "a threat to the national security and foreign policy of the United States". The American administration has on several occasions accused the Libyans of being involved in terrorists acts, for example the bomb explosion in April 1986 at the La Belle disco in West Berlin, which killed three people including two American servicemen, was declared to be the work of the Libyans. But what little evidence there was about the bombing pointed to Syrian rather than Libyan involvement.

Shortly after the Berlin disco bombing, the Americans retaliated by bombing Tripoli and Benghazi, killing Ghadaffi's 15-month-old daughter and about 37 other Libyan civilians. Many politicians believed this action was not justified, and coined the term 'state terrorism'.

Margaret Thatcher was easily persuaded to back America's anti-Ghadaffi activities because Britain had good reasons of its own to complain about the activities of Libyans abroad. In April 1984, Police Constable Yvonne Fletcher was shot dead outside the Libyan People's Bureau in London by a Libyan holed up inside. But it is significant that Baroness Thatcher did not mention Lockerbie once in her 800-page autobiography, although she discusses the 1986 air-raids on Libya in some detail. Many who read the book were left wondering if she is still convinced of a Libyan connection.

Nevertheless, the Scottish police have brought charges against the two and want them extradited to Scotland to stand trial. In turn, Ghadaffi has consistently refused to allow it, arguing they would not get a fair trial in Scotland or any other part of the United Kingdom.

He has said he will agree to a trial of the two Libyans in a court outside Britain - in the Hague, Netherlands, for example. But the British government insists the trial must take place in Scotland, and so there is a stalemate. Many cannot understand why the British authorities refuse Ghadaffi's offer and wonder whether they are less than confident of a conviction in a neutral court.*

THE LOCKERBIE bombing was undoubtedly a complex operation: PanAm-103 was destroyed by a Toshiba radio-cassette recorder containing probably three hundred grams of Semtex. The relatively small explosion completely destroyed the jumbo jet in mid-air more effectively than a sophisticated air-to-air missile because the suitcase containing the bomb was placed in the forward cargo hold of the aircraft, very close to the fuselage.

Had the suitcase been placed further inside the cargo hold, the other luggage would have shielded the explosion and the aircraft may not have been so fatally damaged. Moreover, the container containing the suitcase was put just beside the place where the delicate electronics of the aircraft were housed. Was this yet another coincidence or careful planning?

It was established that the luggage container with the suitcase was placed on board at Heathrow airport, and some have speculated that the terrorists had one or more accomplices at Heathrow, able to ensure that the suitcase containing the bomb was put in a position where the explosion was likely to bring the plane down. If this is the case, there were almost certainly more than two people involved.

The case against the two Libyans largely rests on the evidence of the owner of a clothes shop in Malta who is supposed to have sold clothes to them, some of which were found in the wreckage. It is alleged they put the clothes into a suitcase and then put the suitcase on an Air Malta flight from Malta to Frankfurt, where it was transferred to a flight to Heathrow and then put on PanAm 103 to New York.

*Libyan agents have been accused of other atrocities during the last decade. A French inquiry blamed four for an explosion on board a passenger flight from N'Djamena, Chad to Paris on September 19, 1989 which killed 171 people.

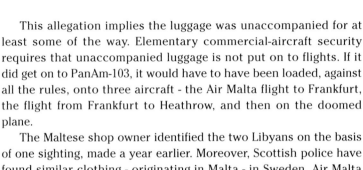

This allegation implies the luggage was unaccompanied for at least some of the way. Elementary commercial-aircraft security requires that unaccompanied luggage is not put on to flights. If it did get on to PanAm-103, it would have to have been loaded, against all the rules, onto three aircraft - the Air Malta flight to Frankfurt, the flight from Frankfurt to Heathrow, and then on the doomed plane.

The Maltese shop owner identified the two Libyans on the basis of one sighting, made a year earlier. Moreover, Scottish police have found similar clothing - originating in Malta - in Sweden. Air Malta denies any involvement with the Lockerbie disaster and won an out-of-court settlement against the British television company, Granada, and the Independent newspaper of London, neither of which could apparently substantiate its story of a Maltese connection.

The other main evidence said to implicate the Libyans in the Lockerbie case involves the timer used to set off the bomb. It was made in Germany by a company run by Edwin Bollier, who first said his timers had been sold only to Libya; only later was it revealed that some of Bollier's timers were sold to the Stasi, the former East German secret service. Bollier has also said two or more timers were probably stolen from his factory in Zurich.

Bollier has suggested in The Observer newspaper of London that the fragment of the timing device found in the Lockerbie wreckage may have been planted by Western intelligence agents to frame Colonel Ghadaffi's regime. Be this as it may, the timer evidence is hardly the independent, indisputable forensic evidence pointing to the Libyans that the authorities claim it to be. Some Scottish legal experts, including the Professor of Scottish Law at Edinburgh University, doubt that a jury would convict the Libyans on this basis and argue that a judge might well throw out the case on the grounds there is simply no case to answer.

If the Libyans are not responsible for the Lockerbie bombing, who is? A number of theories have been put forward. Three of the 107 Americans on board PanAm-103 were secret agents returning to Washington after a CIA operation in the Middle East. It is thought they may have been engaged in a plan to rescue American hostages in Beirut. One of them was Major Charles Dennis McKee, a top US military communications expert. As soon as their presence was known, there were suggestions Flight-103 was blown up to assassinate the CIA team. There is absolutely no evidence for such a theory.

There was also a drug dealer on the aircraft, carrying a substantial amount of heroin. Again, there is no evidence his presence played any role in the bombing.

Some commentators suggested that Iran had hired the Popular Front for the Liberation of Palestine General Command, the extremist Palestinian group, to do the job. This would have been part of an attempt to exact revenge for the shooting down of an Iranian Airbus over the Gulf by an American warship, The Vincennes, in 1988. The Iranian civil passenger airliner, carrying 290 Muslim pilgrims to Mecca, hit the sea and sank in the Straits of Hormuz; 66 children were among the dead. The timing of the two events may or may not be significant: the Iranian Airbus was shot down four days before the main Muslim religious holiday, while The Maid of the Seas was blown up four days before Christmas.

A cell of the Palestinian group was active in Germany around the time of the Lockerbie bombing and was known by the German police to have bombs of a type similar to the one used to destroy PanAm-103. Two months before the Lockerbie disaster, the German security police, acting on a tip from the CIA, raided flats in Neuss and Frankfurt occupied by the Popular Front and captured an arsenal of guns and ammunition. Most significant of all, they discovered a Toshiba radio cassette recorder which had been converted into a triggering device for a bomb. In addition, the police unearthed five kilos of Semtex, six kilos of another plastic explosive, three kilos of TNT, and 89 detonators.

The cassette recorder captured by the police was primed with a charge of Semtex and its electronics had been stripped out and replaced with a timing device connected to a barometric fuse. The device was obviously designed to blow up an aircraft when it was flying at a predetermined high altitude. The lowering of atmospher-

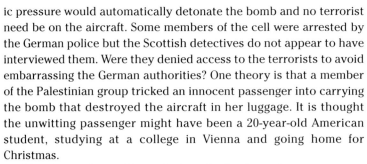

ic pressure would automatically detonate the bomb and no terrorist need be on the aircraft. Some members of the cell were arrested by the German police but the Scottish detectives do not appear to have interviewed them. Were they denied access to the terrorists to avoid embarrassing the German authorities? One theory is that a member of the Palestinian group tricked an innocent passenger into carrying the bomb that destroyed the aircraft in her luggage. It is thought the unwitting passenger might have been a 20-year-old American student, studying at a college in Vienna and going home for Christmas.

After the explosion blew a hole in the fuselage, depressurisation and air friction ripped it apart within seconds. Fragments of luggage were scattered over a 70-kilometre trail, across woods, bogs, hills, and lochs. By virtue of a massive police operation enough fragments were collected to largely reconstruct the container and confirm that it indeed contained a bomb built into a Toshiba radio-cassette recorder. Although this was a different model from the one captured by the police raids in Frankfurt, the fact that a Toshiba radio-cassette recorder was used to blow up the PanAm plane possibly links the Popular Front to the Lockerbie disaster.

The mass murder at Lockerbie will probably go unpunished. If so, the demands of British and American foreign policy will not have helped. The Scottish police, who carried out the most intensive investigation in British police history, must find this state of affairs extremely frustrating. It is also a bitter blow for the families of the people who died at Lockerbie, and who remain in ignorance even of the motives of the culprits.

Chapter Four

NATURE OF THE BEAST

Terrorism has been with us since before Guy Fawkes and the Gunpowder Plot but it still has no satisfactory definition. Were the ANC a terrorist organisation under apartheid in South Africa? Was the Allied bombing of Germany during the Second World War a form of terrorism in that it was designed to intimidate civilians? The authorities may call the perpetrator of violent acts a terrorist, but the terrorist - or, indeed, the people - may regard the person as a freedom fighter for a political cause or religious belief. Yasser Arafat, the leader of the Palestinian Liberation Organisation, put this most succinctly when he addressed the United Nations General Assembly: "whoever stands by a just cause cannot possibly be called a terrorist...".

So which 'atrocities' should be classed as terrorism? Who is a terrorist? Across the globe we can see how those initially labelled as terrorists change into 'freedom fighters' and then democratic leaders, the most famous example obviously being that of Nelson Mandela. For years, the white South African apartheid government hunted-down members of the African National Congress (ANC) as terrorists, and incarcerated Mandela, its leader, in Robin Island, one of the most infamous prisons in the southern hemisphere. Yet despite the opprobrium reserved for the ANC in white South Africa, to black South Africans and their sympathisers ANC members were heroic freedom fighters; and they are now in government. The country is an apt example of how violent means have been used to achieve a political end.

Another is Kenya, where the Mau Mau waged a bitter but successful battle against the British colonisers for Kenyan independence. The British regarded these Kikuyu fighters as terrorists, while the Kikuyu believed that violent revolution was the only way of achieving independence for Kenya. Jomo Kenyatta, one of the leaders of the Kikuyu, was arrested in 1952 and imprisoned by the

British as a terrorist. Released in 1961, Kenyatta went on to become the leader of his finally independent country.

But it is not only governments that have developed out of 'terrorism'. The state of Israel was itself born in 1948 largely because of the activities of the Jewish Stern and Irgun organisations, which must surely prove that in some cases violence pays quite handsomely. The British, driven out of Palestine by such violent acts as the bombing of the King David's Hotel in Jerusalem, labelled the leaders of both organisations as terrorists. But to the vast majority of Israelis they are national heroes - Yitzhak Shamir and Menachem Begin, both of whom later became Prime Ministers of Israel, among them.

So how close can we come to defining terrorism? We usually associate the killing of significant numbers of people with war. Terrorism kills people but is not generally thought of in those terms, perhaps because in our minds it simply does not fit into the recognised spectrum of violence in international affairs.

Terrorism has, however, become a threat to peace and security both nationally and globally yet the international community is loathe to classify terrorism as criminal behaviour or as low intensity conflict. Peter Calvocoressi, a British historian, puts the point well: "Various types of belligerence fit uneasily into an international state system. With the growth of power of the state it has become common to label as war only those kinds of organised violence which are conducted by a state... but there remain further kinds of belligerence, commonly disparaged as terrorism. This is a word to beware of. It has become a term of abuse used to excite prejudice and fuel unthinking reactions - which is all the more deplorable since terrorism does exist and has to be countered."

A major definitional problem is that every government will determine which acts are terrorism according to its domestic and foreign policies. Governments, always anxious to maintain the status quo, often find it politically expedient to call their opponents terrorists; by doing so they hope to win the battle for public support. To this end, some governments classify other countries as terrorist

states. The American and British governments use this term against Libya, for example, even though they do not use it against Saudi Arabia or Israel which are guilty of great violence and state-sanctioned terror. Governments will happily condemn some states while being relatively uncritical about the behaviour of others, simply because it suits their wider foreign-policy goals, such as the economics of the oil and gas industry, or the battle against religious and political fundamentalism: support the lesser evil to prevent a far greater catastrophe.

Governments also pass laws about terrorism without incorporating a definition of the term which adequately covers the different kinds of terrorist activity. Because of this confusion, various other agencies have therefore adopted their own descriptions of terrorism in order to go about their business. According to the FBI, terrorism is: "the unlawful use of force or violence against persons or property to intimidate or coerce a government, the civilian population, or any segment thereof, in furtherance of political or social objectives".

The US State Department, with its foreign policy responsibilities, uses a definition of 'terrorism' with an international dimension: "...premeditated, politically motivated violence perpetrated against a non-combatant target by sub-national groups or clandestine state agents, usually intended to influence an audience. 'International terrorism' is terrorism involving the citizens or territory of more than one country". The Office of Technology Assessment (OTA) of the US Congress adopts a somewhat broader working definition of terrorism: "The deliberate employment of violence or the threat of violence by sovereign states or subnational groups, possibly encouraged or assisted by sovereign states, to attain strategic or political objectives by acts in violation of law intended to create a climate of fear in a target population larger than the civilian or military victims attacked or threatened."

Getting agreement about a definition is further complicated by the frequent use of the word terrorism by totalitarian and authoritarian governments. Military regimes in Latin America, Africa, and

Asia have committed, and many are still committing, terrible atrocities against their citizens by claiming their victims are terrorists and that they, the military, are undertaking legitimate 'counter-terrorism' operations.

Opposing sides may disagree about whether an act should be labelled as terrorist but most people instinctively know what is meant by the term. In his book 'Terrorism and the Liberal State' Professor Paul Wilkinson, a leading expert on terrorism, points out that: "Political terrorism may be briefly defined as coercive intimidation. It is the systematic use of murder and destruction, and the threat of murder and destruction in order to terrorise individuals, groups, communities or governments into conceding to the terrorists' political demands."

The Oxford Dictionary takes a similar view, defining a terrorist as: "Anyone who attempts to further his views by a system of coercive intimidation" and as "a member of a clandestine or expatriate organisation aiming to coerce an established government by acts of violence against it or its subjects". So intimidation using unpredictable violence to achieve a political objective is clearly the key element in terrorist violence. In Paul Wilkinson's words: "What distinguishes terrorism from other forms of violence is the deliberate and systematic use of coercive intimidation".

In practice, then, whether a violent act is or is not called terrorism will depend on who is describing it. But the difference can be crucially important - especially to victims, as there may be financial considerations: a few countries - Israel is one - give financial compensation to victims of terrorism. There may also be insurance implications and there are all too often political considerations. To label a violent act as terrorism, rather than as an ordinary crime, may suit some political purposes, both domestic and international.

Terrorist activity may be either a domestic or international violent action or a series of violent actions. Terrorist activity which spreads across national boundaries - such as the hijacking of an aircraft or an attack on an airport - is often called international terrorism. Violence - whether it involves bombing, attacking individuals or installations, hijacking aircraft, hostage taking, shooting, kidnapping or threatening violence - is, of course, criminal and subversive but its essential character is usually political.

Terrorists may be individuals or subnational groups. Encouragement and assistance for terrorism may come from countries, but they may also be the perpetrators of violence. Other perpetrators may be narco-terrorists (such as the Colombian drug cartels) or single-issue groups, such as anti-abortionists or animal rights extremists - who use terror to pursue a single domestic issue.

Innocent civilians and property are the usual targets of terrorist violence. The terrorists' purpose is to use fear to disrupt the economic, social, and political life of a society: 'Kill one, scare ten thousand' is the modus operandi. Fear is spread by bombings, hostage-taking, assassinations, kidnapping, shootings and murders. By these acts the terrorists hope to achieve their political or religious goals; goals which cannot be achieved by conventional political means. They try to get though bullets and bombs what they cannot get through the ballot box.

TERRORISM dates back to antiquity. It has been used world-wide throughout history, and the names of some of the early terrorists are still used today, such as the Zealots, the Assassins and the Thugs. These early terrorist groups were mainly motivated by religion. Between 66 and 73 AD, for example, a millenarian Jewish group called the Zealots used terrorist violence to fight against the Romans in occupied Judea in Palestine. In a fierce campaign, the Zealots assassinated individuals, killed many people by poisoning wells and food stores used by the Romans, and sabotaged Jerusalem's water supply. But they were just as susceptible to divisions as modern terrorists and also targeted Jews who opposed them.

Between 1090 and 1272 AD, the Assassins, a Muslim Shi'a group, battled with the Christian Crusaders attacking present day Syria, Iran, and other places in the Middle East. They also attacked Muslim

Sunni enemies. If an Assassin was killed during an operation he was guaranteed an immediate ascent to heaven, and this was a seductive promise that some Muslim terrorist groups still use to encourage martyrdom in suicidal attacks.

The Thugs, an Indian religious group of robbers and murderers, operated for no less than 600 years between the seventh and nineteenth centuries, killing, according to Bruce Hoffman of the Department of International Relations, St. Andrews University, between 500,000 and a million people. Unsuspecting travellers were individually strangled as sacrifices to Kali, the Hindu goddess of terror and destruction. By today's standards, the weapons used by these ancient groups were very primitive, mainly swords and daggers. Nevertheless, history has demonstrated their actual methods can work, a lesson not lost on modern terrorists.

Between 1800 and World War I terrorists used bombs and guns to murder many monarchs and government ministers. The assassins were typically driven by left- or right-wing anarchist ideologies. They believed that radical political and social change was best achieved by killing political leaders, kings and heads of state. Some of the most disruptive or influential assassinations were those of Tsar Alexander II on March 13, 1881 in St. Petersburg and the Austrian Archduke Francis Ferdinand on June 28, 1914 in Sarajevo, which brought on World War I, the assassination in October 1934 in Marseilles of King Alexander of Yugoslavia and French Foreign Minister Barthou, and the attempted assassination on February 28, 1887 in St. Petersburg of Tsar Alexander III, the son of Alexander II, by a group which included Vladimir Ilyich Lenin's brother, Alexander.

Terror has also been used, and is being used, by totalitarian regimes as a state policy. Roman Emperors, including Tiberius and Caligula, used terror to deter opposition. So did Robespierre, during the French Revolution in 1793 and 1794, in a reign of terror in which some 20,000 people died. In the nineteenth century, Spanish and Italian anarchists used terrorism. More recently, extreme right and left-wing totalitarian regimes used terror without legal restraints to

achieve ideological ends. Each of Hitler's and Stalin's regimes killed millions of people in concentration camps, in which servants of the state tortured, executed, and worked people to death as a state-condoned policy to force through ideological and economic policies. A number of countries continue to condone such brutalities, although on a much lesser scale. But nowadays we usually associate terrorism with sub-national groups whose aim is to overthrow existing governments or institutions. The mid-1960s saw an unprecedented increase in the frequency of such activity, and terrorism has now become deeply ingrained on modern international life.

AS THERE IS no precise or generally accepted definition of terrorism, statistics about it vary widely, depending on which violent events the compilers choose to include. Numerous data-banks exist, dealing with domestic terrorism, state terrorism, international terrorism, terrorism in specific countries or regions, and so on.

One major comprehensive source of international terrorist events is the RAND-St Andrews Chronology of Terrorism, compiled by RAND, a Californian think tank and the Centre for the Study of Terrorism and Political Violence at the University of St Andrews. Dating back to 1968, it only covers international terrorism involving the citizens of more than one country. Another major source is the database of Business Risks International (BRI), which includes both domestic and international terrorism. It dates back to 1979.

Just how rapidly terrorism has escalated since the end of the 1960s is dramatically shown by statistics published by the Office of Technology Assessment (OTA) of the US Congress, based on BRI data. During the 1970s there were a total of 8,114 terrorist incidents world-wide according to the OTA (an average of about 22 incidents a day). These killed 4,978 people and injured 6,902. In this period terrorists were most active in Europe, the region accounting for 3,598 incidents. Latin America was the next most active region with 2,252 incidents. Then comes the Middle East with 1,097 incidents.

During the 1980s there was even more terrorist violence: a total of 31,426 incidents which killed 70,859 people and injured 47,849. On the average day in the 1980s nearly 200 people were killed and 131 injured. The most violent region was Latin America, accounting for 18,173 terrorist incidents. Europe followed with 4,613, Asia with 4,302, and the Middle East with 3,060. These figures include both domestic and international incidents. The RAND-St Andrews chronology records more than 8,000 international terrorist events since 1968. Of these, 2,536 occurred in the 1970s and 3,658 during the 1980s. A total of 1,975 people were killed by international terrorists in the 1970s; this total escalated to 4,077 during the 1980s. The region with the greatest number of international terrorist attacks during the 1970s was Europe. During the 1980s it had switched to the Middle East.

Ever since 1968, the most common type of international terrorist attack involved bombings - roughly half of the total. Attacks with other weapons (such as hand grenades, rocket-propelled grenades, and bazookas), fire-bombings, drive-by shootings, and other sabotage accounted for about 20 per cent of the international terrorist incidents. Hi-jackings, assassinations, kidnappings and the taking of hostages account for most of the remainder.

A crucial aspect of international terrorist violence is the way its lethality has increased over the past 30 years. During the 1980s the number of international incidents was about 50 per cent more than in the 1970s; but twice as many people were killed. About one in five of the incidents during the 1980s killed one or more people, but terrorist attacks were directed mainly at buildings and installations rather than directly at individuals or the public. Diplomatic targets accounted for about a quarter of the international incidents since 1968; about another quarter were business targets; about 20 per cent were airlines; and less than 10 per cent were military installations.

A good understanding of the scale and lethality of recent international terrorist violence can be seen in the RAND-St Andrews chronology for 1994, a typical recent year, which records a total of

350 international terrorist incidents - which killed a total of 419 people. People died in 96 incidents and 89 were injured. In ten of them, more than 10 people were killed. In three of these, more than 20 were killed; in one, more than 30 were killed and in one, more than 90 people were killed. In 14 incidents, between three and eight people were killed.

The Middle East was the region with the largest number of international terrorist incidents during 1994: 125. The next most violent region was Europe, with 92 incidents. Latin America accounted for 58; Sub-Saharan Africa for 39; Asia for 28; and North America for 5. One hundred and twenty-one of the international terrorist incidents during 1994 involved bombings. Seventeen of these killed people: a total of 215. Eighty-six incidents involved other attacks on installations; 23 of them killed a total of 106 people. During 1994, 56 of the incidents involved kidnapping; in eight of them people were killed. Another 46 involved assassinations, killing a total of 73 people.

A few of the incidents in the 1994 RAND-St Andrews chronology indicate the variety of international terrorist attacks which take place. The first incident of 1994 happened in Angola on the 2nd of January: six mortar bombs were fired at the American-owned Chevron oil production facility, injuring one person. The Front for the Liberation of the Cabindan Enclave claimed responsibility. On 16th January, a typical terrorist kidnapping took place. Two American missionaries were kidnapped by FARC in San Jose, near Villavicencio in Columbia to protest against the presence of American Army engineers in Columbia. The bodies of the missionaries were found a year and a half later in Cundinamarca Province; they had been shot.

One of the most lethal international terrorist incidents recorded by the RAND-St Andrews chronology for 1994 occurred in Hebron, Israel on 25th February. A Jewish West Bank settler, a member of the extreme right-wing Kach group, entered the Ibrahim Mosque at the Cave of the Patriarchs in Hebron and opened fire with an automatic rifle on the congregation worshipping inside. He killed 39 Arabs and wounded 250 before committing suicide. A lethal bomb-

ing of an aircraft took place in Panama on 19th July when an explosion ripped apart a Panamanian commercial aircraft just after it had taken off from Colon. All twenty-one people on board, most of them Jewish, were killed. A Lebanese suicide bomber was suspected and the group Ansar Allah, Warriors of God, claimed they were responsible. This group also claimed 'credit' for the bombing, on 18th July, of a building in Buenos Aires, Argentina, which housed a number of Jewish organisations. The bomb was also detonated by a suicide bomber.

A dramatic series of incidents took place in March, when the IRA fired four mortars on Heathrow Airport in West London. The mortars were buried in the ground just outside the perimeter of the Airport and fired by remote control. The mortar shells were not primed, presumably deliberately, so they did not explode. On 11th March, the IRA fired four more mortar shells at Heathrow Airport from a different location. Again, the mortar shells were not primed and did not explode. On 13th March, the IRA fired four more mortar shells at Heathrow Airport from yet another location. Once again, the shells did not explode, but the attacks made a mockery of the security forces attempts to capture the IRA and proved that even the world's busiest airport was extremely vulnerable to terrorist attacks.

We can conclude that whereas up to the end of the 1960s the perpetrators of terrorism were those fighting for the independence of their countries from colonial rule, most modern terrorism arises from bitter religious, political, ethnic, cultural, nationalistic, and ideological conflicts. When states use or encourage terrorism they usually do so as part of a regional power struggle.

JUST AS it is not possible to find a satisfactory definition of terrorism by sub-national groups, it is not always possible to classify unambiguously violent acts committed by states. In some cases, a country may claim a violent act which it has committed is an act of war whereas others may argue the country has committed an act of terrorism. In fact, so far as nations are concerned, war and terrorism overlap. A definitional problem is that countries often become involved in violence when they do not regard themselves to be in a state of war. The armed forces of a country may, for example, be fighting guerrilla groups who regard themselves as 'freedom fighters' battling against an oppressive regime.

An obvious example is the fighting between the military forces of the old South African apartheid regime and the military wing of the African National Congress (ANC). The South African government did not in those days claim to be at war; instead the government said it was fighting an illegal 'criminal'/terrorist/guerrilla organisation; the ANC said that it was fighting to overthrow a regime which because of its oppression had no legitimacy. To describe such conflict in a country which claims to be at peace the term low-intensity conflict is often used.

Another example of a sub-national group describing itself as a nationalist group fighting for independence against a government which dismisses it as 'terrorist' is the Basque Fatherland and Liberty (ETA) group, founded in 1959. ETA is fighting the Spanish authorities to create an independent homeland in the Basque region of Spain. ETA can claim some success in that limited home rule was granted to the Basques in 1982. Some countries engaged, or expecting to be engaged, in low-intensity conflict use specially trained commando units to fight it. These troops are generally allowed to operate without the normal constraints of the law: they assassinate people on the other side, capture and torture them, and chase guerrillas across borders in hot pursuit. This 'illegal' violence can be described as state terrorism.

Another definitional problem is that a country may sometimes sponsor and support a sub-national terrorist group by providing it with money, weapons, and explosives and by training its members. Earlier in this century, the Bulgarian government and Italy's Fascist government under Benito Mussolini, for example, supported such groups as the Croatian Ustashi. Since the mid-1960s a number of countries have been accused of aiding sub-national terrorist groups including: China, Cuba, Iran, Iraq, Kuwait, Lebanon, Libya,

Nicaragua, North Korea, Saudi Arabia, Sudan, Syria, the former South African regime, the former Soviet Union, and the former communist regimes of East European states. As described earlier, Libya has supported the IRA by supplying it with weapons and explosives and training its members; it has also supported ETA. Iran and Sudan sponsor Islamic Fundamentalist groups, Syria sponsors Palestinian groups who combat Israel, and so on. There are also examples of countries actually employing a sub-national group to commit a single act of terrorism in pursuit of some domestic or foreign policy goal.

ON APRIL 15, 1986 American aircraft from Sixth Fleet aircraft carriers and from airbases in Britain, bombed targets in the Libyan cities of Tripoli and Benghazi. The attack was in retaliation for alleged Libyan complicity in the bombing of La Belle discotheque in West Berlin, a favourite haunt of American servicemen, on 5th April 1986. Three people were killed in the disco bombing, two of them Americans. On 17th April - in reprisal for the bombing of Libya - two kidnapped Britons and an American were murdered in Beirut.

Although the Reagan Administration accused Libya of being behind the disco bombing, and the explosion on 16th April 1986 of a TWA airliner travelling from Rome to Athens which killed four Americans, the evidence for Libyan responsibility is controvertible. On the basis of the evidence, Syria, which is known to have been involved in terror attacks in Europe at the time, is just as likely to have been involved in both events as Libya. But President Reagan was obsessed with Colonel Ghadaffi. Libya was undoubtedly supporting acts of international terror from the late 1970s onwards and, in 1982, the White House tried to persuade America's allies to impose economic sanctions on Libya, but the efforts failed. At the end of 1985, Reagan stated that Libya was a 'threat to the national security and foreign policy of the United States'. In January, 1986, all Americans living in Libya were instructed to leave the country. In March, the American conflict with Libya escalated. The American

Navy held manoeuvres in the Gulf of Sidra, a disputed area. On 24th March 1986, the Libyans fired missiles at US Navy fighters flying over the Gulf of Sirte. In retaliation, the Americans bombed a Libyan missile base and patrol boats. The US ended their manoeuvres on 27th March. Nine days later the Berlin disco was bombed and after another ten days Tripoli and Benghazi were bombed.

The American bombing of Libya was not supported by many of America's allies. The main support came from Britain and this was probably more due to Prime Minister Thatcher's close relationship with President Reagan than to anything else. Be this as it may, the British allowed American bombers stationed in the United Kingdom to take off and bomb Libya.

The targets in Tripoli and Benghazi were supposed to be attacked with precision-guided munitions. But many bombs missed their targets and civilians were killed. In particular, four one-tonne bombs fell on Bin Ghashir, with devastating results. Ghadaffi's private residence was attacked, although he was not there. His children, however, were, and the bombs killed his fifteen-month old daughter and injured two of his other children, aged three and four. Television pictures of dead and injured children and other civilians casualties flashed around the world bringing condemnation down on the Americans. About 40 people were killed and 90 injured in the attack; the exact figures have not been published.

This one American action killed more Libyans than all the alleged Libyan terrorist attacks had killed Americans. The question raised was: Who are the terrorists - the Libyans or the Americans? And the term 'state terrorism' was coined.

So can the American bombing of Libya be justified under international law? Conor Gearty, senior lecturer in law at Kings College, London, has this to say: "The justification under international law claimed for its actions by the administration was 'self-defence'. However, acting so as to prevent the occurrence of imminent violence falls under the category of self-defence, whereas punishing some one for having done something falls under the category of retribution or retaliation. President Reagan's action belonged to the

second of these categories, not the first. The only defence claim that could be raised was in retaliation to some unspecified type of violence against unspecified victims in some unspecified place at some unspecified time in the future."

The fact that most American and European politicians and commentators did not at the time roundly condemn the American bombing as an act of international terror shows the gross inconsistencies in the use of the word 'terrorism'. As Gearty says, the Americans escaped being categorised as terrorists: "for the same reason as Israel invariably does: their violence was authorised by a government and was executed by the official armed forces of a state. The reward for using their full power in this way - with all the greater efficiency in terms of killing that it implies - is to have the label 'terrorist' rendered inapplicable to them".

The Rainbow Warrior sets sail to protest against French nuclear tests.

If the roles had been reversed and Colonel Ghadaffi had decided to bomb Washington to defend Libya from further American attacks he would undoubtedly have been condemned as an international terrorist. The fact that the Americans did not move against Syria, which supported international terror acts as much as Libya did, can be explained by Syria's relative strategic importance in the Middle East. Libya was sufficiently weak to allow the Reagan Administration to work out its frustration for seeming to be incapable of respond-

ing to terrorism. The Americans would have thought twice about moving against a country more capable of responding militarily to an attack on it or a country more important for strategic or foreign policy reasons.

THE CLASSIC EXAMPLE of state terrorism must be the French bombing of a Greenpeace ship in New Zealand in 1985. Details of this tragedy show how easily the security services of a major Western nation were misused.

Photographer Fernando Pereira, was killed aboard the Rainbow Warrior when two French time-bombs were detonated.

In 1978, Greenpeace bought a rusty 418-tonne, 44-metre long trawler Sir William Hardy and rechristened it the Rainbow Warrior. After many journeys of protest, against, among other things, the dumping of radioactive waste at sea and the ocean transport of highly radioactive spent fuel elements from nuclear-power reactors, the vessel was fitted with sails and renovated at Jacksonville, Florida, USA.

On March 15, 1985 the ship left Jacksonville for what was to be a 32,000-kilometre expedition, stopping in Hawaii, the Marshall Islands, Kiribati, Vanuatu, and New Zealand before going on to the Moruroa Atoll, in the Pacific, to protest against a series of nuclear-weapon tests which the French planned to conduct there. The Moruroa protest was the main purpose of the expedition. From Jacksonville, the Rainbow Warrior sailed for Honolulu where she picked up Fernando Pereira, a Dutch-Portuguese photographer who was to document the voyage, and headed for the island of Rongelap in the Marshall Islands. A number of American nuclear weapons had been tested in the atmosphere close to the Marshall Islands and Rongelap had been seriously contaminated with radioactive fall-out

from the nuclear explosions. The Americans had assured the inhabitants of Rongelap that it was safe to live on the island, but the islanders were convinced that their homes were unfit for human habitation. They were so concerned about this that Jeton Anjain, the Rongelap representative in the Marshallese parliament, asked Greenpeace to send the Rainbow Warrior to Rongelap to evacuate the entire population of the island to the island of Mejato, 195 kilometres away, which was less contaminated.

The ship arrived at Rongelap on May 17, 1985 and over a period of ten days made four round trips to Mejato, carrying about 300 Rongelapese and 100 tonnes of their possessions and supplies to a new life in a place more acceptable to them. Fernando Pereira's pictures made sure that the event was witnessed by the world's media. The Rainbow Warrior then set sail for Auckland, New Zealand.

On July 7, she made her way to Marsden Wharf in Auckland, warmly welcomed by members of Greenpeace New Zealand. It was no secret the main purpose of the voyage was the protest at Moruroa. In fact, Greenpeace had sent a telegram to French President Francois Mitterand informing him about the protest. And along the route the world's press had shown considerable interest in the expedition.

Clearly, Greenpeace's protest at Moruroa would focus the world's attention on France's nuclear activities in the Pacific. Such publicity was just what the French did not want: they wanted to carry out their nuclear-weapon tests as secretly as possible. The French were, and, as the publicity and protests surrounding the French series of nuclear tests in 1995 showed, still are, extremely sensitive about independence movements in France's Pacific territories. Knowing this, Greenpeace did not inform President Mitterand that the Polynesians would join the protest, launching their canoes from the Rainbow Warrior into the sea around Moruroa. But the French found out in another way. By old-fashioned espionage.

Sometime before the Rainbow Warrior reached New Zealand, a French secret-service agent, Frederique Bonlieu (real name Christine

Gabon), had infiltrated the Greenpeace office in Auckland posing as a supporter. As part of her work, she answered the telephone, read telexes, and messages from the Rainbow Warrior, in other words, she found out about the movements of the ship and the plans for the expedition to Moruroa.

Using the excuse that she had friends who were coming to New Zealand on holiday, Christine Gabon sent maps of the area and photographs of beaches and harbours to bosses in Paris. She also find out where underwater equipment could be obtained. Her purpose was to assist teams of French secret agents who had been instructed to go to New Zealand and sink the Rainbow Warrior.

The first team arrived at the northern tip of New Zealand by yacht - the Ouvea. Three agents of the Direction General des Services Exterieurs (DGSE), the French secret service, were on board: Gerald Andries, Jean-Michel Bartelo, and Roland Verge. Accompanying them was Xavier Maniguet, a doctor specialising in emergency treatment for people injured in car accidents. This team was to smuggle explosives, diving equipment and an inflatable dinghy into New Zealand.

A second team of agents - Major Alain Mafart and Captain Dominic Prieur - arrived at Auckland airport, using the pseudonyms Alaine and Sophie Turenge, a Swiss honeymooning couple. They hired a camper van which they used to collect the gear brought in on the Ouvea. Colonel Louis-Pierre Dillais, the head of the operation, arrived the following day. Early in July another French spy arrived in Auckland. He introduced himself to Greenpeace people as Francois Verlon, and claimed to be a pacifist. Two other agents arrived in Auckland on the same day as the Rainbow Warrior, bringing the total number of secret agents on the operation to at least ten. Given that New Zealand and France were friendly nations, the size of the group of French agents sent to New Zealand for a hostile purpose is quite extraordinary.

The French spies must have reported back to Paris about the enthusiasm being shown in Auckland for the Greenpeace expedition to Moruroa and the size of the 'fleet' assembling in Auckland to

accompany the Rainbow Warrior to the Atoll. This information about the scope of the protest against the French nuclear tests must have further worried the French government.

On the evening of July 10, 1985 the French agent Jean-Michel Bartelo, travelling in his team's inflatable Zodiac dinghy, tied up at Marsden Wharf, close to the Greenpeace ship. He donned scuba gear and swam towards the Rainbow Warrior, carrying two packets of explosives. He fixed one packet on the top of the stern tube housing just forward of the propeller; the second one he fixed to the outer wall of the engine room. Bartelo then started the timing mechanisms before swimming back to the inflatable dinghy. He left the dinghy on the shore and drove off in the camper van which his colleagues Mafart and Prieur had left parked at a convenient spot.

At 11.38pm, about three hours after Bartelo planted the bombs on the Greenpeace ship, the first one exploded. Several of the ship's crew and photographer Fernando Pereira were relaxing in the ward-room, having a drink. The explosion sounded like 'a thud' but it was powerful enough to lift the people in the wardroom off their seats. One of the crew, Edward Achterberg, thought the explosion had come from the engine room and went to look. What happened next

The wreckage of Greenpeace's Rainbow Warrior after French secret service agents blew it up in 1985.

is described in the Greenpeace report of the sabotage: "dashing into the engine compartment he saw a hole the size of a car in the Warrior's side through which water was pouring at the rate of six tonnes per second. As the Warrior keeled over, Willcox (Peter Willcox was the ship's captain) ordered everyone off the ship. The doctor on board, Andy Biedermann of Switzerland, went to check the cabins and pulled the cook, Margeret Mills, to safety. Gotje went below frantically searching for his girlfriend Hanne Sorensen; Peireira, too, rushed down below, perhaps to get his valuable cameras, which were on his bunk."

It was soon clear to the crew that the ship was sinking; water coming on to the deck rapidly grew deeper. Then the second bomb exploded. All the crew remaining on the ship jumped onto the wharf, with one exception: the photographer Fernando Pereira - he was trapped below. The rush of water produced by the second explosion engulfed him and he drowned. The blast and fire caused by the bombs destroyed the Rainbow Warrior which sank at the dock.

The death toll could have been much greater. Normally many people would have been asleep on the ship at the time of the explosions. But, as luck would have it, many of them were either up and about the ship or away from it. When it was raised from the harbour bed the public could see the ship's engine room was completely wrecked and that the explosion had blown a huge hole out of the hull.

Who were the guilty parties? It was the first act of terrorist violence in New Zealand and the police began a massive investigation involving nearly 100 police officers. Many members of the public supplied information. Eye-witnesses reported seeing the Zodiac dinghy being launched. Night-watchmen at a boat club saw the French agent in his wet-suit loading equipment from the inflatable into the camper van. Suspecting the man was stealing from yachts moored in the harbour they had taken note of the van's license number.

This enabled the police to trace the van to a rental company and to discover that it had been hired by a couple called Alain and

Sophie Turenge - the aliases used by the French agents Major Mafart and Captain Prieur. The police traced the camper van and when the Major and Captain returned to it they were promptly arrested. They were not the most effective secret agents. The two agents made a telephone call while they were in jail which the New Zealand police soon traced to the French secret service in Paris. The Swiss passports used by the two agents were false. This was more than enough to convince the man in charge of the investigation - Detective Superintendent Allan Galbraith - that there was a strong French connection.

From information given by the public the police established that the two French agents under arrest had met the crew of the yacht Ouvea. The police searched the yacht, which was now moored at Norfolk Island, about 1,000 kilometres away from Auckland, and was about to sail to New Caledonia. When they questioned the crew, the police could find insufficient evidence to arrest them. But the police took samples during their search which, when analysed by forensic scientists, were shown to contain traces of explosives. By this time, the Ouvea had sailed into the blue, never to be seen again.

In France, on August 8, 1985, two weekly magazines, VSD and L'Evenement, accused French agents of sinking the Greenpeace ship. President Mitterand was provoked into ordering an official inquiry into the affair. After a short inquiry, the government admitted that French agents had indeed been in New Zealand - spying on Greenpeace - but denied they had any hand in sinking the Rainbow Warrior.

The Tricot report also admitted that Admiral Henri Fages, then director of France's nuclear test programme in the Pacific, had talked to Admiral Pierre Lacoste, the head of the DGSE, about Greenpeace's proposed expedition of protest to Moruroa. What worried Admiral Fages the most was reports that Polynesians would be joining the protest. On March 1, 1985 the Admiral sent a message to Defence Minister Charles Henru, calling for greater efforts to be taken to "forecast and anticipate the actions of Greenpeace". It turned out the word 'anticipate' would be given a sinister meaning.

On September 17, the leading French newspaper Le Monde stated that Defence Minister Henru and Admiral Lacoste were aware of the operation, and had probably ordered it to be carried out. Admiral Lacoste was promptly dismissed and the Defence Minister resigned. There were even suggestions that President Mitterand himself would have to resign. On September 22, 1985 French Prime Minister Laurent Fabius announced that France was guilty of state-terrorism. The statement was a humiliation for the French government: "Agents of the DGSE sank this boat. They acted on orders. This truth was hidden from state counsellor Tricot [who had conducted the initial report]".

On November 4, 1985 the trial of Mafart and Prieur began in Auckland. The prosecution's evidence was not strong enough to prove murder and arson, nor the placing of the bombs on the Greenpeace ship. So instead of facing a trial for the murder of Francesco Pereira and arson, the two accused agents pleaded guilty to charges of manslaughter and wilful damage. They were sentenced to 10 years on the first charge and seven years on the second, the sentences to run consecutively.

France's act of terrorism was an all-round failure. It humiliated France and it did not succeed in stopping Greenpeace's protest at Moruroa. The mission of the Rainbow Warrior was completed by the ship 'Greenpeace', accompanied by a flotilla of several ships. Not satisfied with sinking the Rainbow Warrior, eight French commandos boarded one of the ships in the flotilla, the Vega, which had entered territorial waters, when it was about 6.5 kilometres from Moruroa, and arrested the crew, which ironically included three of the Rainbow Warrior crew, among them Peter Willcox, Rainbow Warrior's captain.

If France is prepared to countenance such outrageous acts of violence as the sinking of the Rainbow Warrior, we must consider the possibility that in coming years renegade states will sponsor even more deadly acts of terrorism and justify it as being in the national interest. Among senior intelligence officials in Washington at the moment there are whispered conversations about the

dangers posed by Saddam Hussein's stocks of chemical and biological weapons, such as anthrax. According to Madeleine Albright, the American ambassador to the United Nations, Iraq has enough anthrax to "kill every single human being on the planet".

Chapter Five

CYBER-TERRORISM

The most obvious image of a terrorist is a man with a grudge or a 'cause' holding a machine-gun or a remote-control device for a bomb. But new weapons are becoming available, notably the humble computer. The CIA and many other intelligence agencies are only just realising that terrorists could use computers to cause destruction - by launching devastating attacks on a nation's technological infrastructure.

Society has changed beyond recognition within the last 20 years as computers have taken control over large areas of our lives. Many of the day-to-day operations of our most important utilities, such as the electricity, telecommunications and water industries, are controlled by computers. At every level, from supply to requesting payment, computers have control. The result is a critical dependence on technology which is now worrying many academics and defence analysts.

These computers, particularly those in the private sector, are extremely vulnerable to a 'cyber-attack', during which terrorists operating from the relative safety of another country, the Middle East perhaps, would use computers and modems to hack into systems which control such vital functions as the electricity supply for a capital city. They could have the power to shut down the entire system.

The American administration is now realising that with technological dependence comes technological dangers. In July 1996, President Bill Clinton signed an executive order creating a presidential commission that will investigate the scope of the problem and recommend ways to protect those key parts of the national infrastructure that could prove to be attractive targets to terrorists - both foreign and home-grown.

The commission, which comprises 10 leading figures from both the public and private sectors, will release its findings in the

summer of 1997. However the President and his intelligence advisers view the risk of a cyber-attack as being so great that an inter-agency taskforce, led by the FBI, has already begun work to try and prevent a computer-assault.

"Certain national infrastructures are so vital that their incapacity or destruction would have a debilitating impact on the defence or economic security of the United States," Clinton said in his executive order, which was signed on the recommendation of an American Cabinet committee formed after the bombing of the federal building in Oklahoma - which destroyed the myth of America as a nation largely free of terrorism.

Janet Reno, the Attorney-General, headed the Cabinet committee and echoed Clinton's concerns. She said members: "...recognised that future terrorist attacks may not be limited to bombs or other 'conventional' weapons. As businesses, government and individuals increasingly rely on computers to communicate and store vital information, terrorists could use more sophisticated 'cyber' attacks to disrupt the functioning of the nation's critical infrastructures."

The committee believes there are nine crucial areas of government and industry that are at risk and must be protected: electricity, gas and oil, banking and finance, water, transport, telecommunications and the emergency services. According to senior officials within the Justice Department, the Cabinet committee has recognised that cyber attacks could come from a wide range of sources apart from terrorists, including ex-employees, lone computer hackers, criminal gangs and even rogue nations, such as Iraq or Libya.

According to Jamie Gorelick, the American Deputy Attorney-General, the impact of a cyber attack is becoming increasingly apparent. "We're really redefining the nature of threats to our national security," she said. "Those definitely are changing very, very rapidly. It is our clear view that a cyber threat can disrupt the provision of services, can disrupt our society, disable our society, even more so than can a well-placed bomb. What we need is the equivalent of the [World War II atomic bomb] Manhattan Project."

Cyber-Terrorism

In mid-October 1996, Gorelick delivered a blunt speech to a forum on combating terrorism, sponsored by the Council on Foreign Relations. She said the West must develop defences against terrorists with the potential to wreak havoc with "little investment of time or money or personal risk". "Our national well-being rests on an increasingly interconnected infrastructure, our power grids, our telecommunications, our banking system, gas and oil pipelines and transportation system are increasingly linked together."

There are more than 150,000 American military computers connected-up to the global Internet system, every one of them offering a potential entry point for terrorists or spies. Gorelick has testified before the Senate that an attack could come within the next two years and she warned: "We will have a cyberspace equivalent of Pearl Harbour at some point and we do not want to wait for that wake-up call. We are sounding that wake-up call now, and we are trying very hard to ensure that we have structures in place, policies in place, laws in place, relationships with industry in place to prevent such an attack and to deal with one, if one occurs." Other American politicians agree with Gorelick: Senator William Cohen has predicted a "series of electronic Pearl Harbours."

Responsibility for dealing with this threat does not only lie with national governments or, for that matter, NATO or the European Union. Many of the most critical computer networks are owned by corporations who must fend for themselves. According to Gorelick, industry involvement is vital because they own the infrastructure that is most at risk and, if they are not involved, security precautions will not be taken to strengthen defences.

Crucially, Gorelick said, a huge amount of the knowledge necessary both to destroy and strengthen defences is in the private sector. Her concern stems from the knowledge that soldiers are transported along the same railway lines that the public use; or that the American military rely on the same national electricity grid for power as everyone else, and the Pentagon uses the normal Federal banking system when it wants to buy boots or bombs. Perhaps the most alarming statistic of concern to the military is the one which

shows that - even in an age when communications win wars - 95 per cent of all military communications take place using the same telephone networks as civilians.

A RECENT study by the American RAND Corporation has highlighted the possible effects of hackers using computer viruses on technology that controls railways, banks, power stations and air traffic control systems. A hacker - a computer expert who can gain illegal access to another computer by using a modem, either for personal gain or malicious intent - can easily cause devastation, according to every expert who has studied the various possibilities.

In one scenario that is causing concern, an information-terrorist ('infoterrorist') would hack into computers in London, New York or Paris that control the water, gas, or electricity supply. When connected, they would then download powerful computer 'logic bombs' that would destroy the program software. The result would be chaos in the industry being targeted.

"Imagine if that situation is replicated in all the phone, water and electricity companies at once," said an official of the American Attorney-General's office. According to him, commuter trains could be directed onto the same section of line by terrorists who alter crucial codes in railway company control computers; nuclear power plants might approach meltdown after hackers shutdown vital safety-critical computer systems; and planes could crash when hackers make their computers go haywire.

To fully understand the potential destructive power of such terrorist attacks we must consider the fundamental change currently taking place in modern warfare: a development which in terms of impact can be compared to the introduction of the machine-gun or fighter aircraft. Our reliance on technology to fight battles has spawned new types of military science and tactical theory. The name for this strategy is Information Warfare (known as InfoWar or Cyber-Warfare) - defined by the Pentagon as a campaign to seize control of an enemy's electronic information systems.

ACCORDING to Jim Settle, former director of the FBI Computer Crime Division, the next major war will be waged exclusively with information rather than bullets. Where the military now go, terrorists are bound to try to emulate them. He said if he was given 10 good computer hackers he could bring America to its knees within 90 days.

Senator John Glenn said approvingly: "We are rapidly getting to the point where we could conduct warfare by dumping the economic affairs of a nation by computer networks." At least such battles would be fought without bloodshed - where the only physical damage is to a nation's infrastructure and economy. Colonel Mike Tanksley, head of the US Army's InfoWar centre at Fort Belvoir, believes this is a good thing: "You can stop a war before it starts. We think we have a paradigm shift here."

Admiral William Studeman, who retired recently as deputy director of the CIA, listed potential targets "all of which are vulnerable today from outside": telecommunications, financial systems, the stock exchange, the internal revenue system, social security, high-tech databases, strategically important companies, research and development, air traffic control systems and banking.

Banks daily transfer vast sums around the world - more than $1,315 billion, according to one estimate - and until now their technological complexity has helped to secure them from outside attack. The networks were a mixture of new and old computerised operating systems which meant that a hacker could never know quite what system he was trying to penetrate. Now, however, new standardised technology is being introduced throughout the financial world which will make it easier for a computer-intruder to navigate the system he is attempting to enter.

The same problem threatens the world of aviation. Modernisation makes them more vulnerable said Dan Gelber of the US Senate, who has studied plans by the US Federal Aviation Administration to replace ageing air traffic control computers. Gelber spent eight months investigating computer security and discovered that few people - even within the intelligence communi-

ty - are aware of the full extent of the risks posed by computer attacks.

The current director of the CIA, John Deutch, has warned of "very, very large and uncomfortable incidents of cyber warfare" and he told senior Washington politicians: "After the threat from weapons of mass destruction, this [the risk of a cyber attack] is next in priority. The electron is the ultimate precision-guided weapon." "There is a highly classified intelligence estimate that focuses on foreign attacks on the public-switched telephone network system of this country," said Deutch.

The CIA believes such attacks could come very soon, but with the true optimism of every government agency, they also believe that the risks and dangers can be countered by manpower and intelligence. "I feel confident that with the development of both expertise and techniques this will not be an insurmountable problem," said Deutch with Churchillian confidence. "We won't be able to spot everybody or spot everybody quickly. But, with time and with ingenuity, we will do well in defending ourselves."

During a Senate hearing on the problem, Senator Sam Nunn expressed his concern and asked Deutch which countries pose the greatest threat. Deutch declined to name any but claimed the CIA and FBI were keeping track of some preparing for a cyber-attack. But, asked Nunn, what about an individual, or a terrorist group? What are they doing? "That is less certain," said Deutch, "and of course, individual criminal elements or individual hacker activities significantly less."

THE basic weapons for a cyber-terrorist is a computer, a modem and the how-to computer expertise. Unfortunately for those working to prevent such attacks, that knowledge has been widely disseminated, helped by the fact that a number of nations have invested millions in developing an InfoWar capability.

Even those who have not picked up expertise in the military can learn the necessary skills. There have been numerous cases of young computer whizzkids using their machines to hack into sensitive military computer systems, and the number of hackers world-wide is mushrooming. According to the Defence Information Systems Agency (DISA), a computer security arm of the Pentagon, there were more than 250,000 separate attempts to hack into the Pentagon's main computers during 1995, and approximately 160,000 were deemed by the government to have been "successful", although they have failed to fully explain what that meant.

Jack Brock, a director of the General Accounting Office of the US Congress, was more open: "Hackers have stolen and destroyed sensitive data and software. They have installed 'back doors' into computer systems which allow them to surreptitiously regain entry. They have crashed entire systems and networks. At a minimum these attacks are a multi-million-dollar nuisance to defence. At worst, they are a serious threat to national security."

Yet even if a hacker does attack, the victim may never know of the 'assault'. For several years, DISA has been employing hacking techniques in a bid to test the defences of crucial military computers. They call the exercise 'Red Teaming' and the results are alarming. In 38,000 tests over the last three years, they managed to successfully gain access to sensitive computers 65 per cent of the time. Only one in 150 attacks was ever spotted and reported. Robert Ayers, the head of DISA's Information Warfare Division, admitted America is not prepared for an electronic version of Pearl Harbour and that the electronic infrastructure is not safe and not secure.

Computers are almost pathetically vulnerable, and there are hundreds of cases, often put down as innocuous microchip errors, which shut-down anything from railway lines to payroll computers. For example, the American telephone company, AT&T, - one of the largest in the world - suffered an embarrassing incident several years ago when a minor computer bug in software, distributed to telephone switching centres, brought the firm's entire long-distance phone network to a complete halt for nearly ten hours. Other incidents are more mundane, but serve to illustrate the fragility of the systems: for example a farmer severed a fibre-optic cable while he

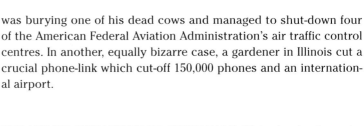

was burying one of his dead cows and managed to shut-down four of the American Federal Aviation Administration's air traffic control centres. In another, equally bizarre case, a gardener in Illinois cut a crucial phone-link which cut-off 150,000 phones and an international airport.

THE ABILITY OF HACKERS TO CAUSE DAMAGE is clearly shown by the case of Julio Cesar Ardita, a 21-year-old hacker from Buenos Aires who used a basic computer in his parent's flat to access top-secret American defence computers. "I've seen inside submarines and much more, I could very easily have wiped out files and rubbed out information," said Ardita in a tape-recorded call he made to his girlfriend that was monitored by the authorities.

Ardita had started his hacking in the spring of 1995, when he used the Internet - the global network of computers - to access computers at Harvard University. From there he 'jumped' into computers at the top secret Los Alamos National Laboratory, the US Navy's Research Laboratory in Washington and its Control and Ocean Surveillance Centre in San Diego; he also hacked into the Jet Propulsion Laboratory at NASA.

Managers at the Naval Command, Control and Ocean Surveillance Centre in San Diego found unusual files in their computers with names such as 'Sni256', 'test', 'Zap' and 'Pinga'. When security officials opened the files, they discovered they contained 'sniffer' programs, which can copy vital information and send it down a modem line to another program: if the user of the host computer changes his or her password, the sniffer program would spot the change and send it by modem to Ardita, so he would still have access to the computer.

When security officials realised they were dealing with a computer hacker, they called in the federal authorities, who were then told by officials from the US Army research laboratories that a hacker had tried to access their computers on more than 90 separate occasions. The investigators traced the sniffer programs back to Harvard

University, where they discovered even more bizarrely-named snif-fer files sitting quietly inside their machines.

The investigators then took out the first-ever court order which allowed them to track down the hacker through the Internet - the cyber-space equivalent of a phone-tap. It was a huge task: with 10 million bits of information flowing through the Harvard computers every second, the team of investigators used a powerful computer to search through every single word looking for just 15 key words which they knew their target (Ardita) had been using. Eventually they managed to track him back to Buenos Aires, where they discov-ered the youngster tapping on his keyboard, and outside their jurisdiction.

The Americans accuse Ardita of accessing sensitive files on radi-ation and aeronautics, and have filed charges against him and applied for an extradition order: "I doubt whether we could success-fully prosecute him, but he could sure help us by giving us information on how he managed to do it," said one federal official. But the hacker's father is none too impressed with American secu-rity precautions: "Obviously the North Americans are not very clear about the security of their systems if a kid from South America can enter it. I would be ashamed to admit it," said Julio Rafael Ardita - a former Argentinean military officer - to The Washington Post.

In this case, Ardita did little actual damage to the computers he hacked. But he is a sign of worse things to come. If he had wanted to, Ardita could have destroyed files or planted corrupted informa-tion. Other hackers have caused millions of dollars worth of damage by destroying crucial files containing research information.

So far, however, few hackers have actually tried to cause damage by destroying programs, such as those which run telecommunica-tions systems. But few doubt there is potential for chaos. For example, in 1994, a German hacker demonstrated to officials from the New York Stock Exchange the ease with which he could take control of the computers that operate the air conditioning system for the exchange. That might not sound particularly hazardous, but the hacker was able to raise the temperature of the exchange, thus

causing the trading systems to fail.

The 'Datastream Cowboy' is another classic example. The hacker, a 16-year-old lad from London, managed to "take control" of the computers of the computer network at the top secret Rome Laboratory, a US Airforce Research Centre in New York. His 'attack' shut-down dozens of computers within the laboratory and cost at least half a million dollars. In a state of blind panic, federal investigators tracked the boy back to his parent's home, and when detectives from Scotland Yard burst through his front door, he realised the enormity of his actions, curled up on his bedroom floor and cried. The boy had managed to steal highly confidential files detailing how US Airforce commanders would relay intelligence and target information in the event of a major war.

The story took a more sinister turn when it emerged the boy had been prompted into his actions by a mysterious "secret agent" (according to sources within the American government) known only as 'Kuji', who the boy never actually met but talked to through the Internet. It is not known if 'Kuji' gave the boy specific instructions or tuition which enabled him to hack into computers which are supposed to be among the most heavily protected in the world, but the scenario troubling the CIA and other intelligence agencies around the world is one of a group of hackers being manipulated by a terrorist organisation, perhaps being threatened into causing destruction via a modem. Such a calamity might already have happened for it is doubtful officialdom would ever admit to having been 'bombed' in this way.

THE AUTHORITIES are only just beginning to investigate the activities of cyber-criminals, but there is ample evidence of a huge degree of criminality going unnoticed and unpunished. For example, investigators have estimated that five international gangs of cyber-criminals have extorted more than $400 million from financial institutions by threatening to destroy their computer systems unless large sums of money are immediately paid into Swiss bank accounts. In Britain more than a dozen banks, investment houses and City broking firms are each believed to have paid up to £13 million to the gangs, but they have not notified the police or publicised the extortion out of embarrassment, and to prevent a loss of confidence in their systems.

According to the director of information technology from one of the largest British banks: "This issue is simply to embarrassing for the industry to discuss openly. No individual company will put their heads above the parapet and admit they have been the victims of computer extortion. Their shareholders would be apoplectic with rage."

THE POLICE therefore have few clues to the identities of the gangs, although they believe that three are American and two Russian. They operate by first obtaining details of the computer system in, for example, a bank. They have done this by sending in an operative to work at the company - as a temporary member of staff, by posing as a journalist from a specialist computer magazine, or as a representative of a market research organisation - and interviewing the head of information technology about the computer systems.

When the gang knows enough to gain access to passwords (the term, according to one security consultant, is "opening the door"), they can hack into the bank and leave coded messages for senior members of staff warning of a computer catastrophe if they don't immediately capitulate. The gangs threaten to download logic bombs, computer programs similar in effect to the most powerful computer viruses, which can be 'detonated' within systems into the bank's computers.

Alternatively, they threaten to use electromagnetic pulses and high intensity radio frequency 'guns' (HIRF) to physically destroy microchips from outside a firm's premises. These devices emit a pulse of energy which is picked up by the circuits inside electronic equipment, burning out the semiconductors or wiping clean the memory chips.

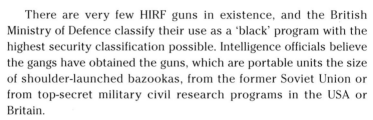

There are very few HIRF guns in existence, and the British Ministry of Defence classify their use as a 'black' program with the highest security classification possible. Intelligence officials believe the gangs have obtained the guns, which are portable units the size of shoulder-launched bazookas, from the former Soviet Union or from top-secret military civil research programs in the USA or Britain.

In several cases, the cyber-gang's coded warnings have either been accompanied by proof of the hackers' power, or by a display: in one case, at a broking house, a ransom of £10 million was paid into a Zurich bank account after coded warnings were left on the bank's computer system and then the entire system was shut-down by the hackers. There was a total computer failure and all stock-market trading was immediately halted.

A security consultant working for a firm which offers advice on computer security to financial institutions has compiled a list of at least 46 separate incidents at banks, broking houses and financial institutions across the Western world. However the British authorities and other intelligence agencies have met a wall of silence when trying to investigate the crimes. According to a statement issued by the Department for Trade and Industry in June 1996: "We are very interested in the allegations of extortion directed at City of London institutions which were brought to our attention in 1994. We responded then by involving many government organisations, including the DTI, the police, the Bank of England and other agencies. So far, we have not been presented with any hard evidence from victims. We would urge those threatened to come forward."

FOR DECADES, the knowledge of how to build and deploy chemical and nuclear weapons has always been available to anyone who really wanted to know. A committed terrorist would do little more than go to his or her public library, where many books and encyclopaedias give quite specific details about the manufacture of weapons of mass destruction. However as terrorism has become more of a threat to democracy, some local governments have taken steps to withdraw such books, or restrict access to them. Now books have been replaced by a new repository for all things extreme: the Internet.

Within seconds of 'logging-on' to the Internet a would-be terrorist can type in a few key words and receive detailed instructions on the manufacturing process and components necessary to build and assemble a basic nuclear device. The bomb would certainly be basic, but its explosive yield would be enough to cause havoc within any town or city.

IT IS SOMEWHAT ironic that the Internet is the favoured place where terrorists or lone maniacs can learn how to commit murderous assaults on society. It was originally designed by the American military to save society in the event of a nuclear war by providing a communications system of last resort. With the system, a message sent from one nuclear strike-force commander to another would try several ways of getting through, bypassing or ignoring any section of line that might have been destroyed by a Soviet nuclear strike.

Since then the system has grown enormously and one can now think of the Internet as the world's largest library and group discussion. It is one lacking in restrictions, access can be entirely anonymous, conducted from the privacy of a bedroom or a training camp in Libya. The very structure and anonymity of the Internet and the World Wide Web (an area of the Internet where users can view 'posters', pictures, reports, films and swap information) lends itself to criminality.

The Internet has become the new communications tool for those who want to avoid the attention of the authorities, including terrorists. Those using it are a diverse community with more than its fair share of oddballs, and at a meeting of the foreign and security ministers from the Group of Seven industrialised nations in July 1996, the politicians agreed on the need for increased regulation.

The need for action was illustrated by the Canadian foreign

minister, Lloyd Axworthy, who described how his 11-year-old son had shown him how to find bomb-making instructions on the Internet. Another good example of the current misuse of the system was made public in 1995, when French government officials asked the American government to take action against an Islamic group based in San Diego that had posted instructions for making and assembling inexpensive bombs on the Internet.

According to Denis Bouchard, a senior Middle East expert working for the French government, the bombs were similar to some detonated on the Paris Metro, and there was concern among the intelligence community that the instructions could encourage other disparate groups to launch attacks against Western targets.

But it is not only a description of the manufacturing of bombs that can be found on the Internet. Simply by swapping a few words upon first entering the 'Net, even a relative beginner can quickly find instructions on how to manufacture chemical and biological weapons that would result in instant death if used correctly.

Internet sites offer advice on the different types of chemical weapons, and discuss the relative merits of, for example, Sarin versus Cyanide, as weapons with which to attack large cities. Complicated chemical equations containing precise descriptions of 'ingredients' for chemical weapons are easily found.

WHAT ARE the politicians doing to prevent the spread of such information? Senior American Congressmen have called for legislation to be passed which would make it illegal to post seditious information such as bomb-making instructions on the Internet. However according to Ian Taylor, the British minister for Science and Technology, governments should "tread warily" before trying to control the Internet. Taylor said it was: "a network of networks of remarkable success, largely because it has grown entirely through private initiative since its original days in the defence sector.

He added: "If it is designed to survive a nuclear attack, it is likely to be resistant to government regulation. But that does not mean to say that there is not a large onus on the network service providers to try to provide a highway code for potential purchasers of software and I'm encouraging them to do that."

The service providers have, however, limited power to police the system. It is by tradition open, so much so that governments are sensitive about being able to 'catch' and read e-mail as it flies across the world from the computer of one individual or organisation to another. Aware of this, renegade computer programmers have made available powerful encryption programs to the wider computer community which make it difficult, if not impossible, for the authorities to decipher information when it is exchanged.

In America for example, friends of Philip Zimmermann, a peace protester and computer expert, have released one of his encryption programs 'Pretty Good Privacy', 'pgp', onto the World Wide Web, enabling anyone to download it for free. Zimmermann once dreamed of bringing down the entire nuclear industry, but then devoted his time to creating computer programs that enabled people to hide from government 'big brothers'.

The computer-world treated him as a hero, because his program secures their electronic messages from interference by governments or criminals. But it works both ways: 'Pretty Good Privacy' is an astonishingly powerful program which works by scrambling a message from a sender and making it illegible to anyone other than the intended recipient with the correct de-coding information; so it is also useful to a terrorist wanting to send secret information to his handlers or other members of his team.

THE FBI confirms the program is among the most secure ever written, and independent experts estimate that de-coding it would require a powerful computer running continuously for ten years. The authorities were so angry with Zimmermann they threatened him with prosecution because under the American Arms Export Control Act the encryption code is classified as a high-technology weapon. Unless a licence is obtained from the federal government,

its export is therefore highly illegal. Zimmermann claimed that it had been put on the Internet for the good of the wider community: "Why should it only be spies who have this sort of technology?" he said.

Chapter Six

HOLY WARRIORS

The spectrum of human violence stretches from individual acts of brutality to a nuclear world war. However the limits of terrorism overlaps at one end with violence by an individual and at the other end with guerrilla warfare.

Guerrillas operate under a military-type organisation that recognises, to some extent at least, the rules of warfare. But terrorists do not operate in these ways and they certainly do not operate according to any recognised rules. Because it is not possible to define terrorism unambiguously there is no agreed list of groups, but using a reasonable definition Bruce Hoffman of the University of St. Andrews identifies about 50 known groups operating today. He estimates only 11 were active in 1968, so there has then been a fivefold increase in the numbers active over the past 30 years.

It is also difficult to classify terrorist groups into various types because many have more than one element. Groups such as the Provisional Irish Republican Army, the Ulster Volunteer Force, the Tamil Tigers in Sri Lanka, Sikh groups in India's Punjab region, among others, have both political/nationalist and religious aims, although in these cases the political element dominates.

Bearing this difficulty in mind, we can identify three distinct types of threat; from an individual; from religious fundamentalists, racists, or millennial terrorism by groups which are becoming more prominent as the year 2000 approaches; and from extreme political groups, both right wing and left wing, and nationalists.

For decades the world has largely had to deal with the last of these. Terrorist groups or organisations had recognisable aims and goals, as well as tightly-knit structures. But as we move through the 1990s, the first two threats are becoming more prevalent. They bring with them a complete lack of respect for the sanctity of life and fluid hierarchies that are proving extremely difficult for the authorities to infiltrate and disrupt.

AN ACT of individual violence can sensibly be called an act of terrorism if the person responsible has a cause of some sort or wants to forcibly 'change society'. Whether the individual concerned should be regarded as a terrorist or simply as maniac is often a difficult question to answer, but the distinction between a terrorist and a criminal is usually obvious. The criminal's motive for his actions are normally purely selfish - for his or her personal gain.

Be they a loner or a maniac, the individual terrorist now has more ability to cause destruction than ever before. Countless attacks across the world, from Tasmania in the southern hemisphere to Dunblane, Scotland, in the north, bear witness to the ease with which it is possible to create lone carnage with conventional firearms. And it is often a small mental step for these individuals to countenance the use of explosives or weapons of mass destruction. From information gleaned through university study or from the Internet, the construction of such weapons as a powerful poison is now perfectly feasible.

A case in point is the 'Unabomber', the nickname given to the terrorist who has waged an astonishing bombing campaign in America for the past 18 years. The evidence suggests that 16 bombings were all carried out by this person. For nearly two decades the terrorist baffled the mighty FBI. Over the years, the bombings killed three people, two of them in Sacramento, California, and injured 23 others. For a short time, the Unabomber's activities shut down air traffic and the mail service on the West Coast of the USA.

Hugh Scrutton was the first to die when a bomb exploded near the 38-year-old's home in December 1985. The next victim was Thomas Mosser, an advertising executive, who was killed in December 1994 by a bomb that was posted to his home in New Jersey. The most recent victim was 47-year-old Gilbert Murray, the president of the California Forestry Association, who was killed in April 1995 when he opened a parcel bomb in Sacramento.

On April 3, 1996, Theodore Kaczynski, a 54-year-old American mathematician and former university professor, was arrested in Sacramento, and he has since been charged with four terrorist bombings. When arrested, he was living in a primitive, one-room cabin deep in the Montana countryside - a recluse from a society he despised.

Kaczynski has been charged with possessing bomb-making materials and with the deaths of Scrutton and Murray. In Kaczynski's cabin the police allegedly discovered a written document which was similar to the Unabombers 'philosophy', which had been published by a national newspaper and Penthouse magazine in an attempt to stop the terrorist bombing campaign. Kaczynski's brother apparently recognised the writing in the document as similar in style to those written by the Unabomber and quickly alerted the FBI. If it had not been for this tip off, it is extremely unlikely the authorities would have ever caught up with Kaczynski.

The Unabomber had a trade-mark that made his attack's unique - each bomb was made "with great love and care", and they were often contained in handmade wooden boxes. His motive was certainly to cause terror but the perverted pride he took in his 'work' was probably another facet of his obsession.

Another lone wolf was Baruch Goldstein, an Jewish-American immigrant to Israel and a settler from Kyriat Arba near Hebron. On the morning of February 25, 1994, Goldstein, a member of the extreme right-wing group Kahane-chai, opened fire with an automatic rifle at Arabs praying in the mosque at the Cave of Machpelah in Hebron - the Tomb of the Patriarchs to Jews, Harm al Ibrahimieh to Arabs - the burial place of the Patriarch Abraham. The Cave is a sacred place for both Jews and Muslims, who revere Abraham as the first prophet. Goldstein fired more than 100 rounds, slaying 29 Palestinians and wounding dozens of others before his gun jammed and he was clubbed to death by survivors.

Dozens of people were killed or injured in rioting which took place after the killings and yet some settlers at Kyriat Arba regard Goldstein as a holy martyr and have set up a memorial to him, complete with an eternal flame. But the motive for the attack, apart from drawing attention to the hatred some extremist Jews have for the Palestinians, has never been properly explained. Some fanatics

will do anything to achieve martyrdom. As is well known, that troubled region was also the scene of an horrific political assassination in November 1995 when Yigal Amir, a fanatical young right-wing law student, breached the supposedly impenetrable security at a Tel Aviv peace rally and shot dead Yitzhak Rabin, Israel's Prime Minister. Amir claimed the killing was justified by religious law because the Prime Minister was wrongly giving up Israeli territory to the Palestinians.

In some cases, a fanatic might make use of a small network of accomplices but the strength of their personality and their independence places them in the category of the lone terrorist. The well-publicised exploits of 'Carlos the Jackal', now in custody in France, is one example. Another who is less well known is Ramzi Ahmed Yousef, one of the most dangerous terrorists this century.

Yousef is held responsible for the bombing of the World Trade Centre in New York on February 26, 1993, which killed six people, injured hundreds more, and confronted Americans with the terrorism threat as no other incident had hitherto done. But intelligence agencies around the world also hold him responsible for an attempt to simultaneously destroy 12 American passenger jets, a bomb attack in Iran which killed 25 people, an explosion on a plane in the Philippines, and plots to assassinate international figures ranging from Pope John Paul II to Benazir Bhutto, the Prime Minister of Pakistan.

> The twin towers of the World Trade Centre form the largest single office complex in the city. The bomb was placed in a large yellow Ryder hire van parked on level B2 of the Centre's underground car-park, near to an area the Secret Service used for storing and parking more than 100 cars and armoured protection vehicles. It took more than seven hours to evacuate the 55,000 people in the tower and they all had to work their way through thick smoke billowing up the stairways - which was the only escape route. Among those 55,000 that day were a large party of young schoolgirls who were trapped in a lift for several hours before rescuers were able to reach them.

After leaving a trail of death in his wake, Yousef and two co-defendants were convicted in September 1996 of plotting a series of explosions on airliners bound for the United States. Such was the level of concern about Yousef's possible level of terrorist support that the US State Department issued an urgent warning to all expatriate Americans of the need for them to increase their vigilance to prevent a possible reprisal attack after his conviction: "The State Department advises Americans travelling abroad that the potential exists for retaliation by Yousef's sympathisers against American interests. While we have no specific threat information, American citizens travelling abroad should pay close attention to their personal security practices in light of the potential threat."

Yousef's case has deeply troubled Western anti-terrorist and intelligence agencies precisely because he represents a new breed of extremist, one with few or no ties and a remarkable propensity towards individual violence directed at the West for what he perceives as its mistreatment of Muslims. According to Oliver Revell, who was in charge of the FBI's criminal investigations division, anti-terrorist agencies have previously been fighting terrorists with an organised structure and an attainable goal such as the reclamation of land or the release of political prisoners. He said: "Ramzi Yousef is the new breed, who are more difficult and hazardous. They want nothing less than the overthrow of the West, and since that's not going to happen, they just want to punish - the more casualties the better." His story therefore teaches much about a new threat which police forces are ill-equipped to tackle.

THE FBI believes that Yousef's real name is Abdul Basit Karim, he was probably born in Pakistan and grew up in Kuwait with his Palestinian mother and Pakistani father. He lived in the tiny Gulf state on and off until 1986, when he flew to Britain to study A-Levels at a college of further education in Oxford. From there he moved across the country to South Wales to study for a degree in computer-aided design and electronic engineering at West Glamorgan

Institute of Higher Education - now known as the Swansea Institute. Yousef returned to Kuwait City after graduating in 1989, and was working in the ministry for planning when Iraqi forces invaded in 1990. Three weeks into the Iraqi occupation he escaped overland, travelling through Iran to Pakistan. Intelligence agents are unclear what he did for the next year, but they believe that in early 1991 he travelled to the Philippines to set-up a base from which he could strike at targets in the Far East.

American intelligence believe he also made contact with Muslim extremists from a group called Abu Sayyaf and one of those extremists, Edwin Angeles, would later betray Yousef to the authorities. "The Philippines became crucial for Yousef," alleges one senior American official. "He met the leader of Abu Sayyaf sometime in early 1992 and together they seem to have plotted a number of atrocities."

After the meeting, Yousef disappeared. Immigration records show he re-surfaced on April 12, 1992, when - using an Iraqi passport - he travelled through Jordan to Pakistan from Baghdad. We then know that on the September 1, 1992 he arrived at New York's JFK airport travelling on an Iraqi passport, and claimed political and religious asylum. Immigration officials allowed him to enter the country, a regrettable decision when one considers that a friend on the same flight was arrested with a false Swedish passport and with luggage containing bomb-making manuals.

For the next six months Yousef lived in various locations around Jersey City with a Palestinian friend who had relatives in Baghdad. Meanwhile, according to the US authorities, Yousef was quietly plotting the attack on the World Trade Centre, contacting other Islamic extremists, buying the necessary chemicals and building a massive 1,500 pound bomb.

Accomplices have testified that Yousef constructed a new design that used urea nitrate, a fertiliser, and ammonium nitrate. Prior to this, FBI explosives experts say it was only used once in more than 73,000 recorded incidents logged in their database. On February 26, 1993 the device was driven into the underground carpark beneath one of the towers and detonated. It caused widespread carnage and destruction but in one respect the attack failed. Yousef had hoped he could make the twin towers topple over by slicing through one of the main support columns. It could have caused the deaths of more than 250,000 people and flattened much of the business district of New York.

WITHIN HOURS of the explosion Yousef was on a plane bound for Karachi but four accomplices, some highly gullible, were arrested within days. One foolishly returned to the Ryder truck company where he had hired the van used to transport the bomb, to demand his money back. The man had used his real name and offered a valid driving licence when hiring the vehicle.

Yousef himself was quickly identified by the FBI as one of their main suspects, but it is a mark of the man's arrogance that he was soon plotting an assassination while on the run. From late July to early August 1993, intelligence officials have discovered that Yousef was hospitalised in at least two Karachi medical centres after a bomb he was making exploded in his face. The FBI and Pakistani intelligence agents believe that Yousef had planned to assassinate Benazir Bhutto and her family by destroying her home in Karachi, probably because he disapproved of a woman leading an Islamic nation.

After receiving treatment Yousef disappeared from view, but has since been identified by a stewardess as the man who sat in seat 26-K on a Philippine Airline flight bound for Tokyo from Manila on December 11, 1994. The man, accompanied by a co-conspirator, disembarked at Cebu, 350 miles from Manila, leaving a bomb under the seat which later exploded - killing a Japanese man and injuring a dozen other people sitting nearby. Miraculously, the pilot managed to control the plane and it made an emergency landing in Okinawa. The authorities believe the bombing was a practise run for the planned simultaneous attacks on 12 airliners, when terrorists would have boarded American-bound flights in the Far East and slipped

miniature bombs under seats. The 12 devices Yousef would have used to murder thousands of passengers were based around a normal Casio digital watch, which was connected to a stabilised type of nitro-glycerin stored as contact lens solution in a nondescript little bottle. The stabiliser looked - to almost any observer - like normal cotton and airline security staff have confirmed that even if the 'contact lens bottle' was put through an X-ray it would not have appeared to be suspect. The terrorists would have walked onto the planes carrying detonators and tiny 9-volt batteries in their shoes, and would then have assembled the entire devices in the lavatories during the flight. They would then have hidden the bombs under the seats and disembarked at the next airport.

On January 6, 1995, police in the Philippines raided a flat in Manila after receiving reports of smoke inside. They arrested one of Yousef's friends and discovered a map tracing the route that Pope John Paul II would be taking when he visited the city a week later. There was also bomb-making material and the authorities found a priest's robe, a fragmentation grenade packed inside a pipe and a timer constructed from the shell of a normal digital watch. One officer found computer disks which gave details of dozens of flight schedules for US airlines.

According to Edwin Angeles the plan involved a suicide bomber dressed as a priest killing the Pope, which would then be followed by the simultaneous airline bombings over the Pacific and, ultimately, another lone suicide bomber flying a small plane loaded with high-explosives - or possibly even chemical weapons - into the side of the CIA's world headquarters at Langley, Virginia. But like a veritable Scarlet Pimpernel, Yousef escaped from the country and returned to Pakistan.

The international intelligence community were by now firmly on Yousef's trail, and special forces counter-revolutionary warfare units were mobilised in the US. Then came the breakthrough the authorities had been waiting for: Ishtiaq Parker, a young South African student who Yousef had been trying to recruit, walked into the American embassy in Islamabad and told US agents where they would find their prey. It is possible the $2 million reward offered for Yousef's arrest played a part in Parker's decision to betray him. With his whereabouts known, FBI agents and Pakistani special forces burst into Room 16 of the Su-Casa guest house in Islamabad and apprehended him. He was flown back to New York the next day.

Yousef was carrying three different passports, each giving him completely different identities. In his hotel room they discovered several remote-controlled toy cars packed with explosives and newspaper cuttings detailing his exploits. He was tried in New York for masterminding 'Project Bojinga', the plan for 12 simultaneous explosions on jumbo jets, and he mounted his own, elaborate defence. Observers noted his handsome features and expressed surprise that this eloquent young man could have committed and planned such atrocities. However, the evidence against Yousef was overwhelming. A Toshiba laptop discovered in the Manila flat, contained details of the plan, and there was a draft letter taking responsibility for the atrocities. They had him "bang to rights", in the words of one jubilant official.

In September 1993, Ramzi Yousef and two others were convicted of the plot. The American government described it as "one of the most hideous crimes anyone has ever conceived", and Yousef is serving a mandatory life sentence. In 1997 he is due to be tried on charges relating to the World Trade Centre bombing - prosecutors are certain to question him about claims he told FBI agent Charles Stern and Secret Service agent Brian Parr, who were taking him back to America after his arrest in Islamabad, that he had considered releasing deadly chemical weapons inside the office building but had dismissed the idea simply because of the cost.

ENSCONCED in New York's Metropolitan Correctional Centre, Yousef remains an enigma. The American authorities may have their man, but in truth, they know little about his motivations, his supporters, his financial backers, his early history, or even his name. Is he Ramzi Yousef? Or is he Abdul Basit Karim, Adam Adel Ali, Adam Khan

Baloch, Dr Richard Smith, Adam Ali, Yousas, Dr Paul Vijaw, Alex Hume, Dr Adel Sabah or Najy Hadd? These are just some of the identities he has used during his travels across the globe.

While Yousef must have had wealthy backers to support him, the FBI believe he is a 'lone gun' who launched himself on a personal vendetta against the West because of his Islamic beliefs, and more specifically, against America: "the Great Satan". In an interview conducted during his imprisonment with a reporter for the Al Hayat Arabic language newspaper based in London, Yousef described himself as an Islamic militant, and said: "I believe this movement, and Palestinians generally, are entitled to strike US targets because the United States is a partner in crimes committed in Palestine."

A number of federal investigators have suggested he could have been acting as an agent of Saddam Hussein, one of a number let loose by the Iraqi dictator on the West with orders to cause as much devastation and destruction as possible in revenge for the Gulf War. There are a number of clues which support this theory, including the fact that the bombing of the World Trade Centre took place exactly two years after the day of the Iraqi withdrawal from Kuwait.

Other evidence includes the fact that one of Yousef's alleged co-conspirators flew back to his family in Baghdad after the bombing and has remained there ever since, and Salameh, another co-conspirator, made more than 40 phone calls to Baghdad during the period between June and July 1992. The FBI has traced most of the calls to Salameh's uncle Qadri Abu Bakr, who spent 18 years in Israeli jails and is known to be a senior official in a Palestinian group backed by Iraq.

Dr Laurie Mylroie, a former lecturer at Harvard University and the US Naval War College who now works with the Foreign Policy Research Institute in Philadelphia believes the evidence of Iraqi involvement is compelling. Dr Mylroie says she has passed her findings to the US Justice Department, but: "They just don't want to hear," she said. In her view, the American authorities stand accused of ignoring unpalatable facts.

RELIGIOUS TERRORISM is the oldest type of terrorism and its 'soldiers' are generally the most fanatical; willing, and even anxious, to die for their cause. For them, an act of violence is an almost divine duty, a response to a God-given religious command. More than any other group, they are the terrorists most threatening future global security because they have no moral restrictions on killing. In the words of Bruce Hoffman, of St. Andrews University, who is an expert on the subject, religious terrorism, or "Holy Terror" as he calls it: "assumes a transcendental dimension, and its perpetrators are thereby unconstrained by the political, moral, or practical constraints that seem to affect other terrorists. "Whereas secular terrorists generally consider indiscriminate violence immoral and counterproductive, religious terrorists regard such violence not only as morally justified, but as a necessary expedient for the attainment of their goals. Thus, religion serves as a legitimising force - conveyed by sacred text or imparted via clerical authorities claiming to speak for the divine."

Hoffman goes on to describe a crucial difference between religious and secular terrorists: they have different constituencies. Secular terrorists appeal to a group consisting of actual or potential supporters, the people who they say they are defending, or the oppressed group they claim to represent. Religious terrorists, however: "are at once activists and constituents engaged in what they regard as 'total war'. They execute their terrorist acts for no audience but themselves. Thus the restraints on violence that are imposed on secular terrorists by the desire to appeal to a tacitly supportive or committed constituency are not relevant to the religious terrorist."

The consequence is that religious terrorists are prepared to commit almost limitless violence against almost any target. In fact, anyone who is not a member of the terrorist's religion or religious sect are valid targets. This means that of all the terrorists groups, the religious ones are the most likely to escalate violence to the use of weapons of mass destruction. The AUM group started this process by its nerve gas attack in Tokyo. It may only be a matter of

time before a religious terrorist group makes and uses a nuclear explosive claiming their devotion to a God as their motivation.

The most dangerous religious (or semi-religious) terrorist groups threatening the future are cults, Islamic fundamentalists and White Supremacists. In the AUM cult we have already witnessed the power a leader can have over his followers: he can inspire or terrorise them to commit any atrocity, even when the individual knows that what he or she is doing is fundamentally wrong. In every country, cults are still largely hidden from public view and the authorities have found it extremely difficult to infiltrate them and discover their motivations and plans.

Part of the difficulty stems from the sheer size of the problem: in Britain, for example, a report published in late August 1996 by the Institute for European Defence & Strategic Studies (IEDSS), warned there are more than 500 cults operating in Britain with approximately 500,000 past or present members. The report, 'The Security of Religious Cults', suggests that an incident similar to the Waco siege in America, when more than 70 cult members died, may soon happen in Britain, and it could also happen in many other parts of the world.

The IEDSS also believes a large number of British cults have the potential to become as violent as the Japanese AUM cult. So how can the authorities monitor these organisations? How do they decide whether a group is harmless? How do they decide whether they have an apocalyptic vision of the future which could lead them to commit extreme violence? It is a difficult judgement for the authorities to make when the real power of the cult is held within the mind of the one or two men (it is almost always men) who 'lead' their followers.

ISLAMIC FUNDAMENTALISTS are responsible for a number of appalling terrorist atrocities in the last few decades, and they conduct their campaigns as a form of Holy War which must not cease until total victory is won. The purpose of their actions is to spread

Islamic law throughout the world, and the late Iranian Ayatollah Khomeini spelt this out very clearly when he said: "We must strive to export our Revolution throughout the world, and must abandon all idea of not doing so, for not only does Islam refuse to recognise any difference between Muslim countries, it is the champion of all oppressed people. Our attitude to the world is dictated by our beliefs."

The even more uncompromising attitude of the Shi'a Islamic Fundamentalists was graphically put by the Mullah Hussein Mussawi, the leader of the Hezbollah terrorists (who was assassinated by an Israeli helicopter raid in Lebanon in 1994): "We are not fighting so that the enemy recognises us and offers us something. We are fighting to wipe out the enemy," he said.

Such fundamentalism has already reached the West. In October 1995 ten people were convicted of plotting to destroy the United Nations building in New York, the Lincoln and Holland tunnels and the George Washington Bridge, in a bid to force the US administration to change its policy towards Israel and the Middle East. The group also planned to kill the Egyptian leader Hosni Mubarak and it discussed kidnapping former President Richard Nixon and the former secretary of state Henry Kissinger. The sentences passed by the court ranged from 25 years imprisonment to life without parole.

Typically such groups are seeking to ensure that Muslims across the world rigidly obey the teachings of the Koran. They also want to ensure that the influence of Western, particularly American, ideas and culture over the Muslim world are minimised. They are vehemently anti-Israeli and anti-American. The Shiite Islamic Fundamentalists believe that the twelfth Imam (the last successor of the Prophet Mohammed) will eventually reappear to "institute the rule of God's law on earth". In the meantime, according to the Shiites, secular governments have no legitimate authority.

For them, Iran is the only country to have started to implement 'true' Islam and is, therefore, the only legitimate country on earth with an absolute duty to work for the universal implementation of Islamic law as defined in the Koran. The use of violent acts is accept-

able and, indeed, an essential means of fulfilling this duty.

To bring home the relative violent nature of Shi'a Islamic terrorist groups, Hoffman points to worrying statistics. "Although these groups have committed only eight per cent of all international terrorist incidents since 1982, they are nonetheless responsible for 30 per cent of the number of persons killed in terrorist acts throughout the world," he said. "Between 1982 and 1989, for example, Shi'a terrorist groups committed 247 terrorist incidents but were responsible for 1,057 deaths."

Hezbollah (the Party of God) is the best known radical Shi'a group (also called Islamic Jihad, the Revolutionary Justice Organisation, Organisation of the Oppressed on Earth, and Islamic Jihad for the Liberation of Palestine) and it operates in Lebanon from the Bekaa Valley, Beirut, and near the border with Israel. It has several thousand supporters and has established cells in some Western European countries, Africa and a few other countries. As is well known, it is closely linked to Iran.

Hezbollah has been involved in many attacks against American targets, including the destruction of the US Marine Barracks in Beirut in October 1983 by a suicide truck bomber, and the bombing of an annex to the US Embassy in Beirut in 1984. It was also responsible for kidnapping and detaining most of the American and Western hostages held in Beirut.

But the widespread use of violence as the means to an end is not confined to Shi'a Fundamentalists. A minority of fundamentalist Sunni Muslims are equally uncompromising in their beliefs and actions. A senior Sunni cleric, Imam Sheikh Ahmad Ibrahim, for example, has allegedly made this 'call to arms': "Six million descendants of monkeys [Jews] now rule in all the nations, but their day, too, will come. Allah! Kill them all, do not leave even one." The Covenant of the Islamic Resistance Movement, usually called by its Arabic acronym 'Hamas', is committed to fight Israel to the bitter end: "Israel will exist and continue to exist until Islam will obliterate it".

But Israel also has its Jewish messianic groups which believe that indiscriminate violence is justified to attain their ends. In July 1983, for example, Jewish terrorists attacked an Islamic College in Hebron, killing three students and wounding 33 others. In 1984 a group of Israeli religious militants, members of the Gush Emunim radical settlers' movement, were imprisoned for planning to blow up the Dome of the Rock (Al Aqsa) Mosque on the Temple Mount in Jerusalem, with the apparent aim of provoking a religious war between Muslims and Jews that would force the Jewish Messiah to intervene.

RADICAL RIGHT-WING American groups share with Islamic Fundamentalists common arguments to justify and legitimise terrorist violence on the basis of their religious beliefs. In the US the right-wing comprises a variety of such movements including the Ku Klux Klan (the best known), Neo-Nazi groups, Christian White Supremacists, militias, such as those implicated in the Oklahoma bombing; and fundamentalist 'Christian Identity' groups. It is feared all will become more violent and more threatening in the next few years. Studies show there are 150 American militia groups, spread across more than 30 states, and more than 100 right-wing local radio stations supporting them.

The various groups which comprise Christian Identity all preach a virulent anti-Semitic, white supremacist theology. The most important are factions called Aryan Nations and The Order (or the Silent Brotherhood), a splinter group. They vilify Jews and non-whites as the children of Satan, and believe that America is the 'Promised Land' where white Anglo-Saxons, not the Jews, are the 'Chosen People'.

Many have a messianic belief in the Second Coming of Christ (a white Aryan Christ, of course), and consider violence to be a crucial

"A well-regulated militia being necessary to the security of a free state, the right of the people to keep and bear arms shall not be infringed."
-Second Amendment, the United States Bill of Rights.

element in their 'campaign': "You're damn right I'm teaching violence," said the elderly Reverend William Potter Gale, the founder of the Christian Identity movement during a speech in the 1980s on a radio station in Dodge City, Kansas. "God said you're gonna do it that way, and it's about time somebody is telling you to get violent, whitey."

White supremacists and militias have, according to the authorities, already laid complicated plans for a massive assault on the federal government. For example, at a gathering of American white supremacists at Hayden Lake a decade ago, according a federal grand jury indictment, plans were announced for the violent overthrow of Washington administration and the creation of a separate Aryan nation within the United States. The indictment charged that the white supremacists planned to "carry out assassinations of federal officers, politicians and Jews, as well as bombings and polluting of municipal water supplies." During a raid on a white supremacist camp in Arkansas after the Hayden Lake incident, police and FBI officers found large amounts of cyanide that were allegedly destined to be used for the pollution attack.

In recent years, their propensity for violence has made further headlines, and rendered the Hayden Lake meeting prophetic. Randy Weaver, a Christian Identity member, barricaded himself inside a cabin near Naples, Idaho. Federal Marshals had been watching for 18 months and Weaver's 14-year-old son and his wife were shot in a gun battle with the authorities; a Federal marshal was also shot.

The siege was a forerunner of the 1993 Waco incident, where federal officers laid siege to the Branch Davidian sect. Agents tried to storm the buildings which quickly led to mass bloodshed when the wooden buildings caught alight. It led to an urgent re-examination of militias supported by thousands of disaffected Americans.

On June 18, 1984, in Denver, Alan Berg, a Jewish radio talk show host, was assassinated by members of The Order. In 1983 and 1984, members of The Order had carried out a number of terrorist acts of violence in their war against the US state apparatus dubbed the "Zionist Occupation Government" or 'ZOG' including two murders and several robberies. This terrorist campaign was based on the strategy detailed in The Turner Diaries, a novel widely regarded as anti-Semitic which spelt out an apocalyptic vision of a race war in the United States and a nuclear world war. At the end of the book, terrorists belonging a group called The Order capture America's nuclear weapons and use them to destroy a number of American cities, and then to attack Israel and the former Soviet Union. Published in 1985, the book is still avidly read by white supremacists in the United States, perhaps because its apocalyptic vision is so close to their own beliefs.

Jeffrey Kaplan, a leading expert in right wing violence in the United States, explained their extraordinary ideas: "Doctrinally, the movement placed its primary stress in the so-called two-seeds doctrine... the Bible was held to be the history of only one people, the descendants of the race of Adam, the true Israelites who are in reality the white race. The Jews represent a separate creation - the result of the seduction of Eve by Satan..."

Many of Christian Identity's ideas became the orthodoxy of the extreme right in America. Those following it mainly came from conservative Protestant churches. Christian white supremacists are also generally opposed to any form of government above the level of local government. This 'anti-big government' doctrine is combined with a belief that the administration in Washington, the financial centre in New York, and the American media, are all controlled by Jews. Their main purpose is therefore to overthrow the 'ZOG'.

This explains why many on the American radical right put great store on survivalism, the maintenance of arsenals of weapons and training in their use. They consider the right to bear arms a crucial element of the constitution. But any level of violence, even a nuclear world war, would be welcomed by some white supremacists as a means of eradicating the groups they hate and to fulfil their aim of creating a white-only world.

To prepare for this day some are accumulating stocks of food and are training to survive a nuclear of biological holocaust.

Concern heightened when a man, who police discovered had a membership card for the Aryan Nation group, was arrested in Ohio in 1995 for procuring three vials of bubonic plague by mail-order from a micro-organism repository. The man is alleged to have given false laboratory code numbers to the American Type Tissue Collection, a charitable organisation which serves as a national store

The aftermath of the Oklahoma bombing - one of the worst atrocities ever committed on American soil.

for thousands of micro-organisms. The man had also obtained samples of Yersina Pestis, a disease which wiped out more than a third of Europe during the fourteenth century. "We just don't know how to stop these people," said one FBI agent based in Washington monitoring the rapid growth of white supremacists.

US politicians took prompt action and voted to make acquiring human pathogens (lethal bugs) 'under false pretences' a federal crime. Senator Orrin Hatch, a Republican from Utah, pointed out that until then: "The only limits on who may buy human pathogens are those imposed by the sellers themselves."

The catastrophe of the bombing of the federal building in Oklahoma brought home to the American authorities and the public that radical militias were a force to be reckoned with. After Oklahoma, on June 14, 1996, a group called The Freemen, another anti-government militia, surrendered after holding out for 81 days on a ranch in Jordan, Montana, surrounded by 100 or so FBI agents. Fourteen of the last group to leave the ranch were accused of threatening to kidnap and kill federal officials and taking part in a $1.8 million cheque fraud scheme. Seven are accused of assisting federal fugitives to avoid arrest.

The American militias are not new but their sheer numbers in recent years have taken the authorities and the police by surprise. However, the authorities have had some notable success in preventing further atrocities. In July 1996, federal agents in Arizona raided the home of a member of the 'Viper' militia who stood accused of plotting to blow up government buildings. The agents discovered nearly 300 kilos of ammonium nitrate, a key bomb ingredient, as well as more than 70 machine guns. John Magaw, the director of the federal Bureau of Alcohol, Tobacco and Firearms, said officials also discovered blasting cord, and warned emphatically: "Terrorism has come to the United States."

Evidence obtained by a police officer working undercover showed that the Viper militia had constructed powerful bombs and made training videos describing the best spots to plant high-explosive to destroy federal buildings. Janet Reno, the US Attorney

General, confirmed intelligence reports that the suspects had been planning to devastate federal buildings, including the offices of the FBI, Internal Revenue Service, the Secret Service, National Guard and police departments.

In another militia incident in early October 1996 the federal authorities arrested seven people with close connections to the Mountaineer Militia of West Virginia on charges of plotting to blow up a new $200 million FBI fingerprint centre. According to a senior FBI agent: "They [the arrested suspects] appear to have been trying to prevent the completion of the facility because they believe it will enable us to keep a better track on them. And they are right, that's exactly why we need it. They're fighting a terrorist guerrilla war against the very existence of our democracy, and we need all the help we can get."

The Oklahoma bombing showed the entire American nation it was vulnerable to an attack from forces operating within its own borders. The huge blast - twice the size of the largest IRA bombs - killed 168 people, injured hundreds more, and put a new name on the list of world terrorist atrocities to match those of 'Lockerbie', 'Munich' and 'Enniskillen' for sheer barbarism.

But the perpetrators of the bombing of the Alfred P. Murrah federal building in Oklahoma, on the 19th April 1995, were not - as originally thought - Arab terrorists working in America. Instead, the authorities blame clean-cut white boys who served in the US armed forces. Timothy McVeigh and Terry Nichols both had links to militia organisations, and both had renounced the authority of the federal government.

The aftermath of the bombing, which left a crater eight feet deep and 30 feet long, was broadcast live on TV. The tiny bodies of children attending a day-centre were carried out in the arms of fire-fighters, whose tears and emotions were clearly visible to viewers. The state governor, Frank Keating, recounts a snatched conversation he had with one member of the emergency services outside the nine-storey building on that fateful day: "You find out whoever did this. All I've found in here are a baby's finger and an American flag," said the man.

Chapter Seven

REBELS WITH A CAUSE

Terrorism targeted at political or nationalist objectives, the third category identified in the last chapter, has proved remarkably resilient to democratic change around the world. Violence by such groups has grown rapidly since the 1960s. Since the late 1980s there has been further growth in right-wing terrorism committed by groups which are often racist and hold bizarre political views.

Right-wing groups usually use violence more indiscriminately than those on the left but in terms of the numbers killed, the conflicts between left-wing groups and military and security forces in Latin America have been the most lethal. Tens of thousands of people, many of them innocent victims, have been slain in the name of some form of Marxist ideology.

In Europe, large numbers of civilians have been killed in the conflict between a Kurdish group (the PKK) and the Turkish government. The PKK, Partiya Karkeren Kurdistan - the Kurdish Worker's Party or Apocus, is a Marxist group of Turkish Kurds. Founded in the mid-1970s, it aims to set up Marxist state in south-east Turkey, a region containing a large number of this ethnic group. The PKK has at least 3,000 active combatants and some thousands of supporters, and pitches itself mainly against Government forces in south-east Turkey. Fighting has been, and is, extremely fierce. Over the past 20 years, more than 13,000 people have been killed.

It is also active from time to time in Western Europe and it battles with rival Kurdish groups. In 1986, the PKK attacked a NATO establishment in Mardin, Turkey. It has also kidnapped Westerners but released them more or less unharmed. Assistance probably comes from Syria, Iran, and Iraq, which offers 'safe havens'.

Devrimci Sol (Dev Sol) is another left-wing terrorist group operating in Turkey since 1978, mainly in Istanbul, with the aim of staging a national revolution. Up to the early 1980s, it attacked Turkish,

American, and NATO targets, with bombings and assassinations. The group, which had several hundred members including a few dozen armed militants, was then considerably weakened by the arrests of large numbers of its members. It re-emerged in the late 1980s, assassinating active and retired Turkish military and security officers. In the early 1990s, it resumed attacks on foreign targets, and was responsible for more than 30 bombings of Western diplomatic, cultural, and commercial buildings.

In Greece, radical left-wing groups have been committing terrorist attacks for the past 20 years. Epanastatikos Laikos Agonas (ELA), or the Revolutionary People's Struggle, emerged on April 29, 1975 by firebombing eight cars belonging to American servicemen in the military base at Elefsina. Its aim is to provoke a Marxist-Leninist revolution. Ironically, it began its operations shortly after the military junta in Greece was dismembered and Konstantinos Karamanlis became the Prime Minister on 24th July 1974 in a restored democracy.

ELA is thought to have about 30 active members all opposed to capitalism, imperialism, fascism, the USA, and the United Nations. It also opposes Greek membership of the European Union and NATO, and has targeted American military and business installations. Since 1986 it has also attacked Greek government targets, mainly bombing buildings. In 1990 the ELA tried to broaden its support by announcing an alliance with a revolutionary organisation called '1st May', which was first heard of in 1987 when it tried, but failed, to assassinate George Raftopoulos, the then President of the Greek General Confederation of Labour. On January 23, 1989 the group assassinated a public prosecutor.

The alliance with 1st May dramatically changed ELA tactics. In about 200 terrorist attacks made by ELA before the alliance - all bombings - there were no casualties. But on February 26, 1992, ELA and 1st May used remote-controlled explosives to blow up a bus carrying Greek riot policemen, seriously injuring 18 of them. Then on September 19, 1994, a remote-controlled device was used to blow up another Greek police bus, killing a senior policeman and injuring ten colleagues and three civilians. It seems the alliance with 1st May has turned ELA from a group which took care to avoid causing casualties into a terrorist group which, in the words of George Kassimeris, an expert in Greek terrorism: "will strike without warning and without regard to the safety of innocent bystanders."

Epanastatiki Organosi 17 Novemvri, or 'Revolution 17 November', was founded in 1975, named after the November 1973 uprising of students protesting against the Greek military junta. The students had occupied the Athens Polytechnic Institute and on the night of November 16 the junta sent riot troops and tanks to remove them. The exact number of casualties is not known, but at least 34 students were killed and 800 injured in the attack.

Public horror at the police brutality hastened the downfall of 'The Colonels'. 17 November are a Marxist group: anti-American, anti-Turkish and anti-Nato. Like ELA, they are opposed to Greek membership of the European Union and hostile to the presence of American military bases in Greece. Although 17 November probably has no more than 15 members, operating mainly in the metropolitan area of Athens, it is a serious threat to civil order: "For the past 20 years [to 1995] the group has carried out 94 attacks, striking at will against carefully selected and often heavily protected targets," said George Kassimeris.

"Twenty-one people have been assassinated, ranging from US diplomatic and military personnel to Greek politicians, publishers, policemen, magistrates, leading industrialists and Turkish diplomats," said Kassimeris. Astonishingly, however: "in all this time successive Greek governments have been unable to capture any member of the group. Further, not one member of 17 November has been killed in an operation or as a result of actions by the Greek security forces. Nor has any undercover agent ever succeeded in penetrating the group and the astronomical financial rewards offered by the Greek authorities to informers have come to absolutely nothing."

IN LATIN AMERICA the Peruvian terrorist group Sendero Luminoso (Shining Path) is one of the world's most ruthless terrorist groups. Shining Path was formed in the late 1960s by Abimael Guzman Reynoso, a university professor, and it has about 3,000 combatants. Its aim is to destroy by violent means existing Peruvian institutions and replace them with a peasant revolutionary regime, although it has developed extensive links with the narcotics industry.

Shining Path wants to rid Peru of all foreign influences and has engaged in particularly violent forms of terrorism from its bases, which are mainly in rural areas. Since 1986 Shining Path has been extending its reach into urban centres, attacking nearly all the foreign embassies in Peru as well as foreign businesses, foreign aid projects, and Peruvian government and commercial targets.

Another group operating in Peru is the Tupac Amaru Revolutionary Movement (MRTA), a traditional Marxist revolutionary group formed in 1983 and led by Nestor Serpa and Victor Polay. It wants to eliminate foreign influences from Peruvian life and establish a Marxist regime in Peru, and to this end it supports the Bolivian National Liberation Army (ELM), a Marxist group which claims to be the successor to the group established by the famed revolutionary Che Guevara in the 1960s.

MRTA has about 1,000 combatants and is responsible for more anti-American attacks than any other group in Latin America: it has bombed the US Consulate and attacked American businesses and Mormon churches; in 1991 it attacked Peru's Presidential Palace and even President Fujimori's aircraft. The conflict between the Peruvian military forces, on the one side, and Shining Path and MRTA, on the other side, has killed more than 28,000 people since 1980, an indication of the extent of the violence in that troubled nation.

But the violence in South America is not confined to Peru. A number of other radical leftist terrorist groups operate on the continent, including: the Nestor Paz Zamora Commission (CNPZ), named after the late brother of President Paz Zamora, which has operated in Bolivia since October 1990; the Revolutionary Armed Forces of Columbia (FARC) established in 1966 as the military arm of the

Colombian Communist Party; the Emanuel Rodriguez Patriotic Front (FPMR) founded in 1983 as the armed wing of the Chilean Communist party; the Lautaro Youth Movement (MJL) which became active in the late 1980s in Chile; the Morazanist Patriotic Front (FPM) founded in the late 1980s in Honduras; the National Liberation Army (ELM) of Bolivia; and the National Liberation Army (ELN) formed in Columbia in 1963. The conflict in Columbia involving the Colombian government military and security forces, on one side, and FARC and ELN, on the other side, has been particularly lethal, killing a total of about 30,000 people.

IN ASIA, the New People's Army (NPA), the armed wing of the Communist Party of the Philippines, is a Maoist group established in 1968 to overthrow the Philippine government by armed struggle. In addition to guerrilla warfare in rural areas, the NPA has used urban terrorism to further its aims, and has made numerous attacks, using squads called 'sparrow units', on government officials, police and army officers in Manila and other major cities. NPA members also attack Americans involved in the Philippine government's counter-insurgency operations. The NPA has as many as 10,000 fighters and the conflict between them and the Philippine armed forces has so far cost approximately 21,000 lives.

Japan has spawned a violent terrorist organisation which belies the country's relatively peaceful image. On May 30, 1972, three Japanese men travelled on an Air France flight from Rome to Tel Aviv. When their luggage arrived at the baggage hall they extracted machine guns from it and opened fire on the people around them, throwing hand grenades into the crowd at the same time. This indiscriminate attack killed 28 people and wounded 70. The gunmen were members of a terrorist group called the Japanese Red Army (JRA). In the attack at the Tel Aviv's Lod airport, they were operating for the PFLP. During 1974 the JRA and PFLP combined again in attacks on targets in Singapore, Kuwait, Amsterdam, and Paris.

The JRA is an international terrorist group which broke away

from the Japanese Communist League Red Army Faction in about 1970 - its aim is to help the formation of a world government. With links to left-wing terrorist groups in Japan, such as the Anti-War Democratic Front, it aims to overthrow the Japanese government and monarchy. With about 30 active members the JRA has had close links with Palestinian terrorist groups, particularly the Popular Front for the Liberation of Palestine (see later), and has been based in the Syrian controlled areas of Lebanon. The JRA was most active up to 1980, hijacking two Japanese airliners in 1973 and 1977, and attempting to take over the American Embassy in Kuala Lumpur in 1975. After the mid-1980s it carried out several rocket and mortar attacks on a number of American Embassies.

SOME LEFT-WING GROUPS have renounced terrorism in favour of normal political activities, for example the Terra Lliure (Free Land), a Catalonian separatist group formed in the 1970s with the aim of establishing an independent Marxist state in the Spanish provinces of Catalonia and Valencia. The group made minor bomb attacks against property in north-east Spain, including foreign banks and travel agencies, but in July 1991, the leaders announced that the group had stopped terrorist activities.

The Farabundo Marti National Liberation Front (FMLN), an El Salvadoran umbrella organisation composed of the Central American Workers' Revolutionary Party (PRTC), the People's Revolutionary Army (ERP), the Farabundo Marti Popular Liberation Forces (FPL), the Armed Forces of National Resistance (FARN), and the Communist party of El Salvador's Armed Forces of Liberation (FAL), reached a peace agreement with the government of El Salvador on December 31, 1991. The FMLN had a total of about 6,500 combatants and carried out a range of terrorist activities in the 1980s, supported by Cuba and the Nicaraguan Sandinistas.

Left-wing terrorist groups come and go and it is sometimes difficult to judge whether or not they are likely to return to violence. One of the archetypal 1970s terrorist organisations, the German Red

Army Faction (RAF) is not currently active but may become so again even though many of its top leaders have been arrested.

The small but highly disciplined RAF is the successor to the Baader-Meinhof gang, which originated in the German student protest movement of the 1960s. Its ideology is a mixture of Marxism and Maoism, and it was responsible for a number of assassinations, kidnappings, robberies, and bombings. It operated with about 15 members but they were supported during their heyday by several hundred supporters who provided logistic support; further backing during the early 1980s came from the German Democratic Republic.

The First of October Anti-fascist Resistance group (GRAPO) is another small Maoist terrorist group, with less than 12 members operating in Spain. GRAPO is said to have had links with the French group Action Directe, the Italian Red Brigades and the German RAF group. GRAPO, established in 1975, carried out small-scale bombing attacks on American and NATO facilities in Spain, including the bombing in 1991 of a railway line outside Madrid and the bombings of segments of the NATO pipeline in Spain. The group has been considerably weakened by the arrest of some of its members, and only time will tell if it becomes active again.

Also unclear is the current status of the Armenian Secret Army for the Liberation of Armenia (ASALA), a Marxist group formed in 1975 to compel the Turkish government to admit publicly that it has some responsibility for the deaths of 1.5 million Armenians in 1915, pay compensation, and give territory for a homeland for the Armenians. Its leader, Hagop Hagopian, was assassinated in Athens in April 1988. ASALA mainly attacked Turkish targets using bombings and assassinations, but little has been heard of the group since Hagopian died.

THE TERM 'EXTREME RIGHT', when applied to terrorism or anything else, is, like the term 'extreme left', hardly precise but there really is no better alternative. Although left-wing terrorists are prepared to commit indiscriminate violent acts, most appear to believe

that the ideal society is a non-violent one run by co-operation rather than conflict. Right-wing terrorists, however, generally believe that conflict and violence are essential elements in society and should be encouraged.

Left-wing terrorists usually spend all their time in secret, underground groups, being chased by the authorities, living under the constant threat of arrest. Most right-wing terrorists, on the other hand, only spend a small fraction of their time committing violence; they are very much part-time terrorists. In America, extreme right-wing groups are greatly influenced by religious fundamentalist movements, and there is a similar situation in Eastern Europe, Israel, Japan, and South Africa, where extreme right-wing ideologies are enmeshed with religious fundamentalism. In Western Europe, however, right-wing extremism is generally secular in nature.

Tore Bjorgo, a Norwegian anthropologist who has done much research into right-wing violence and terrorism, describes the common basic issues and values of the extreme right: "Authoritarianism, anti-communism and socialism, anti liberalism, militant nationalism, racism/xenophobia/anti-Semitism, intolerance towards minorities, Golden Age myths, a particularist (as opposed to universalist) morality, and the notion of violence as cleansing force."

Paul Wilkinson, Professor of International Relations at St Andrews University, explains that right-wing extremists "view their enemies not simply as misguided opponents but rather as sub-human, people who should be accorded a subordinate and degrading status, not only legally but in every aspect of life as well. They blame their enemies for all the ills and injustices in society and are willing not only to demonise them and make them into scapegoats and pariahs, but also to countenance the expelling or even killing of them."

The most influential revolutionary right-wing terrorist movements are the Fascist and Nazi movements which were extremely active throughout Europe in the 1920s and 1930s. Violence and terrorism were essential elements of the Fascist and Nazi ideologies

and as is well known they attracted millions of supporters in the period between the World Wars. The defeat of Germany and Italy in the Second World War and the horror of the Holocaust almost eliminated European Fascist organisations, but somehow the ideas survived and now small groups of neo-Nazis and neo-Fascists have resurfaced in Europe, spawning small violent terror groups mainly in France, Germany, Italy, the Netherlands, and Sweden.

As Ehud Sprinzak, Professor of Political Science, Hebrew University, Jerusalem, points out, the violence and terrorism of these extreme right-wing groups: "which seems to have come in unsystematic waves, has included desecration of Jewish cemeteries and synagogues, vandalism and arson, violent attacks on foreign workers in Europe, fire bombing of shelters housing foreign asylum seekers, rare assassinations and occasional spectacular bombings of public places such as the 1980 Munich Oktoberfest, the Italicus Express in Bologna and a Jewish synagogue in Rue Copernic, Paris."*

In the 1970s, there were violent clashes between neo-fascists and new left demonstrators. But since the mid-1980s, radical right violence and terrorism have been focused on foreign workers and asylum seekers, particularly in Germany. Sadly, job insecurity in Western Europe and public resentment of foreign workers and immigrants, particularly those from the Third World, have significantly increased the confidence and power of the extreme right.

*Sprinzak classifies right-wing terrorism into six general, but not mutually exclusive, types: revolutionary terrorism, reactive terrorism, vigilante terrorism, racist terrorism, millenarian terrorism and youth-counterculture terrorism.

The aim of what is known as reactive terrorism is to restore the earlier status quo and is resorted to by groups which have lost their positions of power in society or fear they may do so. Reactive terrorism is usually applied against organisations which themselves have reached power through the use of violence and a good example is the terrorism conducted by the Organisation Armée Secret (OAS) established in 1961 by the French in Algeria in an attempt to stop the French authorities granting independence to the Algerians.

Vigilante terrorism is used by individuals and groups who believe that the government does not adequately protect them from violent groups or individuals and that they must protect them-

selves. Sprinzak explains that, since the 1960s, the military and police in Latin America have used vigilante terrorism to an unprecedented extent. When they found they could not suppress left-wing terrorism through the ordinary legal system, police and military officers decided to take the law into their own hands and eliminate the left-wing themselves. Using death squads, they killed hundreds of people, particularly in Argentina, Brazil, El Salvador, and Guatemala.

MOST RIGHT-WING terrorist groups believe that certain groups of people are inherently inferior. The archetypal racist terrorist group is the Ku Klux Klan in the USA. Although the Klan is now only a very marginalised group, racist groups are still alive in America and, as we have seen, there are still plenty of white supremacist groups eager to claim the Klan's mantle.

In the 1960s and 1970s, a number of anti-Communist paramilitary and survivalist groups emerged in the USA, mainly as a consequence of the Vietnam War, and some members of these groups committed acts of violence. During the 1980s and 1990s, there has been a considerable increase in the number and interaction of white supremacist groups with strong religious and millenarian inclinations.

Millenarian terrorism is used by religious groups which believe that as we approach the millennium the 'end of the world is nigh', and that only the people who are spiritually prepared will be saved. Interest in millennialism is increasing mainly because of the growth of Protestant Fundamentalism, particularly, but not only, in North America, which anticipates the imminent end of humanity.

Fundamentalism is not only increasingly influential in a religious context but is playing a greater role in political issues, including domestic ones such as abortion. Some millenarian groups have leaders who are prone to violence, and they resort to violence as a reaction to aggression, or perceived aggression, from others which pushes them into a corner. In Sprinzak's words: "So much hate, alienation and desperation are experienced by the group that on

occasions, and after specific incentives have been created, it will resort to terrorism. The occasional shift to terrorism implies the group's inability to fully seclude itself and sever all contacts with organised society." Some American Christian Identity groups - with racist, anti-Semitic, anti-Federal government, and religious fundamentalist beliefs - have been responsible for terrorist violence in the 1980s and 1990s.

Youth counterculture terrorism is right-wing violence carried out by alienated youth gangs and has increased considerably in recent years. Many of these young people shave their heads and are known as Skinheads or simply Skins - others are associated with football hooliganism. In rebellion against middle-class values, they glorify violence, using it against minorities: Jews, left-wingers, homosexuals, and even the disabled.

Skinhead 'culture' began in Britain during the 1970s, but adherents are now found across Europe, including countries in Eastern Europe and the ex-Soviet republics, and in the USA. The Skinheads are often associated with neo-Nazi groups, acting as their 'military-wing', and they have proved to be extremely unpleasant: shootings, beatings, and stabbings have frequently led to the death of victims.

The scale of such attacks is worrying: in Britain alone, the Home Office estimates there are more than 130,000 racially-motivated crimes a year including 32,000 violent assaults.

One notorious Skinhead attack took place in Mölln, near Lubeck, Germany on November 23, 1992, when a couple of local Skinheads set fire to two houses, killing a Turkish woman and two girls and wounding several others. In 1992, neo-Nazis and Skinheads carried out more than 2,000 attacks against foreigners in Germany, including more than 700 cases of arson, killing 17 people and injuring 2,000 others.

A typical example of a neo-Nazi Skinhead group are the notorious Combat 18, a small but ultra-violent British group organised on paramilitary lines. The '18' in its title relates to Adolf Hitler's initials, which are the first and eight letters of the alphabet. Formed in 1992, to 'deal with' hecklers at right-wing British National Party meetings,

it openly advocates violence and attacks anti-Fascists, left-wing demonstrators and Jews, and often provokes violence at football matches. The police believe it was involved in the violence at an international football match between Ireland and England in Dublin in February 1995.

MOST TERRORIST GROUPS with specific political aims are usually nationalist, often formed with the aim of creating an independent homeland. Typical examples of such nationalist groups are the Provisional IRA, Basque Fatherland and Liberty group (Euzkadi ta Askatasuna or ETA as it is usually called), the Tamil Tigers, and groups, such as Al-Fatah, within the Palestinian Liberation Organisation (PLO).

The aim of ETA is to create an independent homeland in the Basque region of north-east Spain and the south-west of France. The population of the Basque region of Spain is about 2.25 million people, of which nearly 70 percent are native Basques, a separate people with their own culture and language. The Basques are famous for their native artists, including Picasso, and their fierce opposition to Franco's fascism during the Spanish civil war and the consequent barbaric bombing of the city of Guernica.

ETA was founded in 1959 to fight the Spanish fascist authorities for freedom for the Basques. But in 1974, it split into two factions - ETA/Political-Military (ETApm) and ETA-Military (ETAm). Some degree of home rule was granted to the Basques by the Spanish government in 1982, since when ETApm has not been active. It eventually rejected the armed struggle as a means of achieving political change.

ETAm, however, continues to make lethal attacks, convinced that the armed struggle is necessary to achieve Basque freedom. This tendency to split is common in nationalist groups. As Conor Gearty, of Kings College, London, explains: "The path of the genuine terrorist may be littered with minor victories, but the final goal is rarely reached. It is extraordinarily difficult for a group to break out of this trap of its own making. For if it attempts to eschew terror, it will undoubtedly split its own ranks and see a militant wing spin off to continue the fight. This has been the experience of Fatah, the IRA, and ETA."

Gearty argues that if a group, or splinter group, perseveres with terror, the violence gradually takes on a less political air, becoming little more than a type of existential self- assertion, a childlike demand for attention. Where once the plea behind the violence was 'listen to me', with long-running terror groups it eventually becomes the shrill cry, 'I'm still here'. But it is, of course, not only terrorist groups which go on past the date when they become relatively ineffective, no longer fulfilling their original aim. Once any sort of institution has been established it becomes very difficult to disband because it acquires a momentum.

ETA-Military is estimated to have several hundred members. Its main activities are the bombing of Spanish government targets and the assassination of Spanish officials, particularly those in the security forces. It operates mainly in Spain and France but has carried out bombing attacks on Spanish diplomatic and cultural facilities in Italy and Germany. The organisation is highly professional, but ETA bombings are sometimes indiscriminate and often lethal. In 1991, for example, more than 40 were killed and 200 injured in ETA attacks. As with other political groups, alliances have been forged, and ETA is reported to have close contacts with the Provisional IRA, and according to sources within the US State Department, ETA terrorists have received training in Lebanon, Libya, and Nicaragua.

ANOTHER GROUP which wants a separate homeland is the Liberation Tigers of Tamil Eelam (Tamil Tigers). Their aim is to create an independent state for the Tamils in the north and east of Sri Lanka, a country with a population of about 18 million, of which about 20 per cent are Tamil and 75 per cent Sinhalese. The Sinhalese are mostly Buddhists whereas the Tamils are mainly Hindus.

Sri Lanka gained its independence from Britain in 1948 after a

period during which the Tamil minority prospered under colonial rule, holding about half of the jobs in the civil service. After independence, the governments attempted to redress the balance by positive discrimination in favour of the Sinhalese.

This discrimination was naturally objectionable to the Tamils, who had become used to holding key jobs. But there was worse to come: in 1956, the government made Sinhalese the national language, and Tamil demonstrations in protest were suppressed with considerable force. Economic depression at the end of the 1960s and in the 1970s caused increasing tensions between the communities and in 1971 a Sinhalese terrorist group, the JVP, began a violent campaign. A year later in 1972 the Tamil Tigers began agitating for an independent Tamil state.

For a few years they limited themselves to a few assassinations and armed robberies, although in 1975 they killed the mayor of Jaffna, a Tamil town. Then, in 1983, the Tamil Tigers became more violent: thirteen Sinhalese troops were killed when the Tamil Tigers attacked Jaffna - in retaliation the JVP rioted in Colombo, the capital of Sri Lanka, killing about 140 people, mostly Tamils. This violence and counter-violence further split the communities.

It also caused the large Tamil population in India to sympathise with their Sri Lankan brethren and the Indians supplied the Tamil Tigers with weapons and training. By the mid-1980s the Tamil Tigers had matured into a formidable fighting force, undertaking violent acts of terrorism and at the same time conducting military operations which brought a large part of northern Sri Lanka under their control.

The terrorism carried out by the Tamil Tigers escalated in 1986 and 1987, with attacks on buses which killed many Sinhalese, including women and children. Violence reached such a level that the Sri Lankan state was becoming dangerously destabilised, and to establish its authority the government attacked, by land and air, the regions in the north which were under the control of the Tamil Tigers.

This brought in the Indians, who were invited by the Colombo government to send peacekeeping troops. In 1987, the Indians were able to broker a truce between the government and the Tamil Tigers, under which the Tamils were given autonomy over the northern and eastern regions. Moreover, Tamil was given the same status as the Sinhalese language. Under this agreement the government conceded an extraordinary amount to the Tamils, given that they had committed numerous acts of terrorism.

Indeed no government has probably ever gone so far in the face of violent attacks by a minority of its people - but the truce lasted a mere two months: a group of Tamil Tigers were caught smuggling a consignment of arms into Sri Lanka, whereupon the Tamil Tigers called off the truce.

A new campaign of violence followed which was even more vicious than anything which had gone before. The Tamil Tigers fought against rival Tamil groups; they made violent attacks on Sinhalese civilians; they started their military operations and took control of Jaffna once more; and they even fought the Indian troops, inflicting large numbers of casualties. A Sri Lankan government attack to regain control of Jaffna caused large numbers of deaths, and renewed violence by the JVP added to Sri Lanka's already considerable problems. The Tigers soon gained world-wide notoriety for its suicide bombers. In a typical recent suicide attack, a Tamil rebel, with explosives strapped to her body, threw herself in front of a government motorcade in Jaffna on July 4, 1996. In addition to the bomber, the explosion killed at least 21 other people and wounded at least 50, including a government official, women and children.

The level of violence and brutality in Sri Lanka has been greater than that in any other part of the world. It is estimated that the 15-year conflict has killed more than 27,000 people and it has had huge economic costs, virtually wrecking the once considerable tourist trade. The Tamil Tigers are undoubtedly a terrorist group, performing random acts of great violence against civilians. But they also fight as guerrillas, engaging the Sri Lankan military in battle, occupying and holding large areas of territory. It is a tragedy that has all but destroyed a country: Sri Lanka is a perfect example of the way

terrorist violence can wreck the entire structure of a once peaceful and beautiful nation, and there is now evidence the situation is degenerating further. The Cambodian authorities are investigating claims that Tamil Tigers have bought sophisticated weapons in Phnom Penh, including surface-to-air missiles (SAMs) and smuggled them back to Sri Lanka via Thailand.

The New Dehli bomb squad ready for action

THE PALESTINIAN LIBERATION ORGANISATION (PLO) is an umbrella organisation containing a number of individual terrorist groups which carry out armed action. The main groups represented on the PLO Executive Committee are Al-Fatah; the Popular Front for the Liberation of Palestine (PFLP), headed by George Habash; the Democratic Front for the Liberation of Palestine (DFLP); the Arab Liberation Front (ALF); the Palestine Popular Struggle Front (PPSF), headed by Samir Ghosheh; the Palestinian Liberation Front (PLF), headed by Mahmoud Abul Abbas; and the Palestinian People's Party (PPP). There are also important non-PLO Palestinian groups in conflict with Israel. The best known is the Popular Front for the Liberation of Palestine - General Command (PFLP-GC).

These Palestinian groups are generally regarded as terrorists because they are sub-national factions whose members do not work for an official organisation. Israeli security agents commit acts - such as assassinations, kidnappings, shootings and bombings - which, if committed by a member of a subnational-group, would be called terrorist acts. But, because these agents work for a government, they are spared the indignity of being labelled 'terrorists' by the wider international community.

As PLO members join the security forces of the Palestinian Authority they, in turn, will probably no longer be called terrorists. Under the Oslo Accords, a maximum of 12,000 policemen were to constitute a Palestinian security force. But, officially, there are now at least 33,000 'security' personnel in the Ghaza Strip and Jericho and the real figure could be closer to 45,000. Many of these are obviously PLO people - 'terrorists' turned into 'policemen'.

The PLO groups are a diverse lot with a history of in-fighting leading to factional splits. The DFLP, for example, is Marxist which split from the PFLP in 1969. It believes that a Palestine state can be achieved only through revolution of the masses and in the 1980s it occupied a place in the PLO political spectrum between that of Yasser Arafat and that of the very radical groups. In 1991 the DFLP itself split into a pro-Arafat group, headed by Yassar Abed Rabbo, and another more hard-line group headed by Nayef Hawatmeh. The strength of the DFLP is estimated by international observers to be about 500, including both groups. It is located in Lebanon, Syria, and the occupied territories, and has received financial and military aid from Syria and Libya.

DFLP operations have all taken place in Israel and the occupied territories. In the 1970s, the DFLP carried out many bombings, including some brutal operations in Israel and the occupied territories. For example, it was responsible for the massacre in the village of Maalot in Israel. In an attack on a school, 25 Israelis, 21 of them teenage children, were killed and more than 100 injured. Since 1988, the DFLP has been mainly involved in border raids.

The PFLP is a radical PLO group, outside the PLO mainstream and responsible for a large number of violent acts. George Habash, its leader, justified the group's indiscriminate use of violence by

arguing that: "When we hijack a plane it has more effect than if we killed a hundred Israelis in battle. For decades world opinion has been neither for or against the Palestinians. It simply ignored us. At least the world is talking about us now."

The PFLP has a history of operating outside the Middle East, drawing the world's attention to the Palestinian cause by conducting dramatic terrorist actions such as the hijacking of commercial airliners. On a single day in September 1970, the PFLP took control of three airliners flying from New York to Europe, taking hostage a total of 475 passengers. The seizure of a fourth aircraft was attempted but failed. A young female terrorist, Leila Kahled, was arrested; she soon gained the sympathy of the world's youth.

One of the aircraft was flown to Cairo and blown up. The other two were flown to Jordan where they were joined by another aircraft, containing more than 100 passengers and crew. These three aircraft were also blown up. All the hostages were allowed to survive in return for the release of seven Palestinian fighters from prisons in Switzerland. The spectacular blowing-up of the airliners produced much global publicity for the PLO, but King Hussein of Jordan was not amused. On September 17, 1970, the Jordanian army attacked PLO fighters in Jordan and eventually the PLO were expelled from the country. However a militant PLO group, Black September, emerged and its first operation was the assassination of the Prime Minister of Jordan, Wasfi al-Tal.

The newly-formed Black September's most infamous attack took place in September 1973, when eight terrorists entered the Israeli compound at the Olympic Games in Munich, West Germany. They killed one Israeli and took nine others hostage. The Palestinians offered to release the hostages if more than 200 of their comrades in Israeli jails were released. The Israeli government refused to agree and in a gun battle at Munich airport, five of the Palestinians, all of the hostages and a German policeman were killed.

The period between 1968 and 1974 was one of escalating violence between the PLO and Israel, with the PLO making many violent attacks outside the Middle East. Israel retaliated to Palestinian violence by military attacks on targets in Lebanon and by assassinating PLO leaders: Israeli violence and tactics were often difficult to distinguish from the violence of the PLO.

In 1974 the PLO moved to improve its image as an international terrorist organisation. On October 14, 1974 the United Nations General Assembly recognised the PLO as 'the representative of the Palestinian people' and on November 13, 1974 Yasser Arafat delivered a speech to the General Assembly - having been treated in all respects during his visit as a head of state. However not all Palestinian fighters agreed with Arafat's new approach, which focused more on politics than fighting, and some opted to continue the armed struggle.

PFLP fighters, for example, captured an Air France airliner in 1976 and held 103 passengers and crew hostage at Uganda's Entebbe airport. The hostages were rescued by Israeli commandos in an extraordinary military raid, during which seven of the PFLP hijackers, 20 Ugandan troops and an Israeli commando were killed. The PFLP action, together with a number of other attacks, was condemned by the PLO leadership, which was particularly embarrassed by an attack on the cruise ship Achille Lauro in October 1985 and the chilling murder of Leon Klinghoffer, a disabled Jewish American. In December 1988, Yasser Arafat renounced terrorism on behalf of the PLO Executive Committee.

The PPSF, led by Samir Ghosheh, a radical group closely involved with the Syrian-dominated Palestinian National Salvation Front, left the PLO Executive Committee but rejoined it in 1991. The PPSF, with less than 300 members, attacked targets in Israel as well as moderate Arab targets.

Violently opposed to Arafat's policy and the PLO, the PFLP-GC, led by Ahmad Jibril (a former captain in the Syrian Army) continues to support international terrorism. Reported to have several hundred members, and closely allied with and supported by Syria, the PFLP-GC is reported to have several hundred members, and is closely allied to - and supported by - Syria. From its headquarters in Damascus, Syria, and from bases in Lebanon, the group has been

responsible for some dramatic cross-border terrorist attacks on Israel using such novel methods as hot-air balloons and motorised gliders.

Of all the PLO groups, Al-Fatah became by far the most important perhaps because Yasser Arafat was at its head. Al-Fatah joined the PLO in 1968 and within a year Arafat was acknowledged as its leader. In the early years, Al-Fatah was concentrated in Jordan, almost becoming a state within a state. In September, 1970, since known as Black September, the Jordanian army fought Al-Fatah fighters and after a year-long struggle, the group was essentially expelled from Jordan.

Most members took up residence in Lebanon, mainly in Beirut. Israel decided to move against them, and in 1982, Israel invaded Lebanon with the main purpose of destroying the PLO groups, particularly Al-Fatah. But they were not successful. A deal was arranged under which Yasser Arafat and his fighters would be allowed to leave Lebanon. Most went to Tunisia, others dispersed to Algeria, Iraq, and Yemen. But in the interim Beirut and southern Lebanon was all but wrecked by the fighting.

AL-FATAH carried out numerous acts of international terrorism in Western Europe and the Middle East in the 1960s and up to 1974. It also offered training courses to a number of terrorist groups from Europe, Asia, and Africa. It has close political and financial ties to Saudi Arabia, Kuwait and other moderate Gulf States, ties which were disrupted by Arafat's support for Saddam Hussein during the 1990-91 Gulf War. It also received weapons, explosives and training from the former Soviet Union and some former communist regimes in Eastern Europe, and weapons from China and North Korea.

With about 7,000 fighters, Al-Fatah is a formidable fighting force, maintaining several elements organised in military fashion and having intelligence wings. These are normally organised as separate groups. Examples are Force 17 and the Al-Fatah Special Operations Group. Force 17 was formed in the early 1970s as a bodyguard force for Yasser Arafat and other senior PLO leaders, but in 1985 it began making terrorist attacks on Israeli targets. In September 1985 it claimed responsibility for killing three Israelis on a boat in Cyprus and Israeli air strikes followed against PLO bases in Tunisia.

The Al-Fatah Special Operations Group, also known as the Hawari Group after its leader Colonel Hawari (who was killed in a car crash in May 1991), was most active in the mid-1980s when it carried out several attacks against European and Syrian targets. It also attacked American targets, including the April 1986 bombing of TWA Flight 840 over Greece in which four Americans were killed.

The membership of the Hawari group includes some of the former members of the radical Palestinian '15th May' organisation which was disbanded in the mid-1980s. Led by Muhammad al-Umari, known as Abu Ibrahim, 'the bomb man', the 15th May organisation claimed responsibility for many bombings in the early 1980s, including the 1980 bombing of a hotel in London, the 1981 bombings of El Al's offices in Rome and Istanbul, and the 1981 bombing of the Israeli Embassies in Athens and Vienna. It also bombed a PanAm flight from Tokyo to Honolulu in August 1982 which killed a Japanese teenager.

The conflict between the PLO and Israel has been exceptionally violent. Since 1964 at least 12,000 people have been killed, the vast majority of them Palestinians. And the violence continues. As Paul Wilkinson, academic and author of 'Terrorism and the Liberal State,' comments: "The fundamental causes of terrorism lie in the bitter ethnic, religious and ideological hatreds which spawn such brutal violence, and the power struggles and rivalries of states. It is all too evident that the ending of the Cold War, far from heralding an end to such conflicts has actually witnessed their proliferation. Hence all the conditions exist in which terrorism is likely to flourish as a mode of conduct for a long time ahead, perhaps for centuries."

SOME OF THE WORLD'S MOST DANGEROUS TERRORIST GROUPS

Revolutionary Organisation 17 November (17 November)...Greece
Revolutionary People's Struggle (ELA)...Greece
Armenian Secret Army for the Liberation of Armenia (ASALA)
1st of October Antifascist Resistance Group (GRAPO)...Spain
Basque Fatherland and Liberty - Political (ETA/P)...Spain
Basque Fatherland and Liberty - Military (ETA/M)...Spain
Chukaku-Ha (Middle-Core Faction)...Japan
Devrimci Sol (Dev Sol)...Turkey
Revolutionary Armed Forces of Colombia (FARC)...Colombia
Japanese Red Army (JRA)...Lebanon/Syria
Kurdish Worker's Party (PKK)...Iran/Syria/Iraq
Morazanist Patriotic Front (FPM)...Honduras
National Liberation Army (ELM)...Bolivia
National Liberation Army (ELN)...Colombia
New People's Army (NPA)...Philippines
Red Army Faction (RAF)...Germany
Sendero Luminoso (Shining Path)...Peru
Tupac Amaru Revolutionary Movement (MRTA)...Peru/Bolivia
Provisional Irish Republican Army (PIRA)...Northern Ireland
Irish National Liberation Army (INLA)...Northern Ireland
Ulster Volunteer Force (UVF)...Northern Ireland
Ulster Freedom Fighters (UFF)...Northern Ireland
Ulster Defence Association (UDA)...Northern Ireland
Emanuel Rodreguez Patriotic Front (FPMR)...Chile
Lautaro Youth Movement (MJL)...Chile
Tamil Tigers...Sri Lanka

Palestinian groups
Democratic Front for the Liberation of Palestine (DFLP)
Force 17
Hawari Group (Fatah Special Operations Group)
Hezbollah (Party of God, Islamic Jihad)
Popular Front for the Liberation of Palestine - General Command
(PFLP-GC)
Popular Front for the Liberation of Palestine - Special Command
(PFLP-SC)
Popular Struggle Front (PSF)
Abu Nidal Organisation (Black September)
Palestinian Liberation Front (PLF)
Al-Fatah
Popular Struggle Front (PSF)
Palestinian Islamic Jihad (PIJ)

Chapter Eight

POISON

T errorists tend to move to higher levels of violence, particularly when the authorities they are opposing fail to respond to their initial demands. What perhaps begins with stone throwing and street violence might escalate to bombings, assassinations and the hijacking of jumbo jets. Inevitably, one wonders what new dangers might come next.

On March 20, 1995, a cult group called AUM Shinrikyo (Way of Divine Truth) released Sarin nerve gas on the Tokyo underground during the rush-hour. It killed 12 people and injured 5,500. There were no warnings given. Nor were the Japanese authorities presented with any demands.

Army personnel equip themselves to enter the Tokyo metro system following the AUM gas attack in March 1995

No other capital city had ever been assaulted in such a manner and many other governments must have shuddered at the possibility of local maniacs emulating a group of which few had previously heard. The AUM group's contempt for human life and suffering lifted terrorist group's last moral restrictions, threatening all sorts of new horrors to come.

The AUM story is worth telling in detail because many aspects of the case highlight how terrorism is now changing. The incident itself was chillingly simple: ten terrorists, in five teams of two

people, boarded five Tokyo underground trains heading for the Kasumigaseki station in the heart of Tokyo's government. The trains were due to arrive at Kasumigaseki just after 8.10 am, at the height of the morning rush-hour. One of the two terrorists in each team kept watch while the other put a packet containing Sarin nerve gas, wrapped in newspaper, in an overhead luggage rack or on the floor of each of the five trains.

The terrorists then punctured holes in the plastic cover of each packet with a needle carried on the end of an umbrella. The gas spread through the underground trains and leaked into the stations where the trains stopped. Thousands of commuters were overcome by the nerve agent. Two underground lines were shut down and at least 26 stations were closed causing huge panic and social disruption. Even now, nearly two years after the attack, hundreds of Japanese suffer from the after-effects: painful eye injuries, constitutional and neurological problems and post-traumatic stress.

The Tokyo incident followed another mysterious Sarin gas attack in June 1994 in Matsumoto, a small mountain resort north of Tokyo. The gas was released in the open air and drifted through the town just before midnight, slaying or seriously injuring every single living thing within a 100-metre radius. The invisible, odourless gas did not discriminate: humans, dogs, carp in ponds and birds were all wiped out. In one block of flats, where it blew silently through the windows, seven people died where they sat or slept, while the lucky few who survived were half-blinded and choked by excruciating damage to their lungs. Tragically, the police authorities failed to find the perpetrators of the Matsumoto atrocity, encouraging the AUM group to mount an even worse attack nine months later. In is now alleged that at Matsumoto the group had been trying to kill three judges who were close to making a decision on a legal action against the cult. They all survived.

Sarin is 20 times more deadly than potassium cyanide, killing in minutes by attacking and crippling an individual's central nervous system. Only a tiny amount is needed to wreak havoc; a fatal dose is 0.01 milligram per kilogram of human body weight. The only other known use of Sarin since the Germans invented it during the Second World War was when the Iraqi's used it against Kurdish rebels in 1988.

Shoko Asahara, the half-blind head of the AUM cult meets Alexander Rutskoi, former Russian Vice President.

THE AUM GROUP was created in 1986, at Kamikuishiki, a village in the foothills of Mount Fuji. Its leader was Shoko Asahara (original name: Chizuo Matsumato), the 41-year-old half-blind son of the owner of a shop selling mats.

Asahara preached a philosophy based on a blend of Eastern religions but he believed, according to psychologists, that he was God. This idea had come to him while at a school for the blind; he had been taken with Erasmus's assertion that in the land of the blind the one-eyed man is king.

As Asahara's following grew he began to preach that in 1997 an apocalyptic war would destroy society. Many young scientists from top Japanese universities were attracted and the cult started recruiting in Germany, the United States, and Russia. Soon the AUM was regularly broadcasting on Moscow radio stations and it had about 30,0000 Russian members compared with about 10,000 in Japan.

In the ten years between its creation and the arrest of Asahara and other leaders of the group in 1996 for the Tokyo nerve gas attack, AUM established good relations with a number of prominent Japanese politicians, especially with those on the extreme right wing. The group accumulated massive cash reserves, reportedly of some $2 billion, including a hoard of unmarked gold bars identical in type to those found in the raid on, and arrest of, a prominent Japanese politician. A great deal of money came from donations made by members of the sect, who would donate all they owned.

The AUM ran many businesses through which it procured

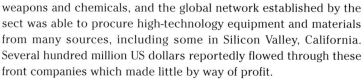

weapons and chemicals, and the global network established by the sect was able to procure high-technology equipment and materials from many sources, including some in Silicon Valley, California. Several hundred million US dollars reportedly flowed through these front companies which made little by way of profit.

During police raids after the Tokyo attack the authorities discovered hidden chambers in the groups Kamikuishiki headquarters which contained tonnes of chemicals used to synthesise Sarin; large

Police raid one of the AUM cult's regional centres in the village of Kamikuishiki. Half-starved members were rushed to hospital

quantities of other chemicals; precision machine tools of the types used to manufacture guns and other weapons, and nitro-glycerine. The police also found a Russian helicopter, recipes for making biological-warfare agents, and an arsenal of weapons.

During one raid of the AUM premises at Kamikuishiki, 50 children were found living in appalling conditions. They were all so malnourished and dirty that the authorities had to wash each one thoroughly

before being able to tell whether they were boys or girls. The children were found wearing 'swimming caps' covered in electrodes and linked-up to batteries attached to their waists. The hats were supposed to channel Asahara's thoughts into their young minds.

It turns out that such mistreatment was also common among the adult members of the sect, who were forced to drink urine, and Asahara's blood and semen, during purification rituals. For this honour they would be forced to pay up to £75,000.

A lengthy inquiry into the affairs of AUM by a US Senate Investigations Committee, with Dan Gerber as its chief council, has found documentary evidence of close connections between AUM

and the Russian security services. The AUM were introduced to top Russian security officials by a prominent Japanese politician and these contacts with Moscow led to AUM members being trained by the Russian army in the use of a variety of weapons including missiles and armoured vehicles. AUM procured a variety of weapon systems from the Russian army, and AUM leaders tried to obtain one or more nuclear weapons from the Russian security agencies. AUM leaders, including Asahara, had made many trips to Russia on procurement missions and established close links with a university in Moscow.

After the 1997 apocalypse predicted by Asahara, the AUM planned to establish a new kingdom. In preparation for this day, the sect was organised as a government into various 'ministries', for finance, defence, and science. By setting its scientists the task of developing powerful weapons, including weapons of mass destruction, AUM was arming itself to prepare for this imminent Armageddon.

As part of its programme to develop nerve gases, AUM scientists set up a test site in Australia. They arrived at Perth airport with crates of chemicals and equipment for a chemical laboratory that reportedly cost £150,000 in excess baggage. Some members were fined for transporting illegal and dangerous chemicals on a passenger aircraft but the cult's objectives were never fully probed.

A testing ground was chosen in the outback region of the Leonora-Laverton district of Western Australia. On June 1, 1993 the AUM purchased the Banjawarn sheep station, and members, including Asahara, moved into the buildings a few months later, vacating it again in May 1994. Members were seen by local people driving around the area in white protective suits and helmets and recent analysis of sheep carcasses suggest the station was being used to test Sarin nerve gas.

Representatives of AUM had already tried and failed to acquire nuclear warheads and advanced laser weapons from the Russian armed forces. They then turned to making their own. Their Australian base gave them the opportunity to investigate the urani-

um concentration in sediment on the edges of local salt lakes. Members flew from sheep station to sheep station in a light aircraft, using monitors to prospect for the material. They even obtained information about the location of suitable lakes from the Australian Mines Department.

It is now known that a party of AUM scientists travelled to Zaire in a bid to obtain samples of the Ebola virus and that experiments were conducted with botulism. AUM also sent scientists to the Nicola Tesla Museum in Belgrade, Serbia, as part of a project to develop weapons that could induce earthquakes using electromagnetic or mechanical waves.

Why did Shoko Asahara mount the Tokyo attack? The answer is not entirely clear but it is known that he taught his followers that if an individual committed enough sins to go to hell then another 'enlightened' person, such as the cult leader himself, could judge that person and pass a death sentence. Members could obtain salvation by killing sinners and anyone outside the cult was a potential sinner.

Asahara was a bully and a torturer who, like many cult leaders, dined on the finest foods while his followers, quite literally, starved. It is unfortunate that the Japanese authorities did not take action against him sooner. Rumours of his brutality were seeping out of the AUM cult for years before the Tokyo subway attack, but little was done. One example of his brutality can be seen in the case of Kotaro Ochida, who worked as a pharmacist at an AUM-run hospital. Ochida had had doubts about the cruel scalding water treatment that was being meted out to a fee-paying patient, and in January 1994, with Hideaki Yasuda, the patient's son (who was also a cult member) he helped the woman to escape. Both were caught and Yasuda was ordered to strangle Ochida.

By early 1995 the authorities were close to launching an investigation of AUM but by then it was too late. Asahara may have decided to order the gassing of the Tokyo underground as some sort of diversion; public prosecutors claimed it was to: "spark massive confusion in the Tokyo area".

The Japanese authorities had many warnings before the Tokyo attack:
On July 2, 1993, dozens of people living near AUM buildings in Tokyo's Koto district complained to the police about suspicious fumes.
On June 21, 1994, seven were killed by Sarin, and many others were injured, in Matsumoto.
In July 1994, mysterious gases caused a number of people living in Kamikuishiki to complain of nausea and severe eye and nasal irritation.
On September 1, 1994, "unknown fumes" resulted in nearly 250 people in western Japan suffering from severe rashes and eye irritation.
In December 1994, the police discovered chemicals believed to be a by-product of Sarin in Kamikuishiki.
On January 4, 1995, AUM accused one of its company presidents of leaking the chemical Sarin into buildings in Kamikuishiki.
On March 5, 1995, fumes were released into an underground train in Yokohama and 20 people were taken to hospital.
On March 15, 1995, five days before the Tokyo attack, three attaché cases containing a mysterious liquid were discovered at another metro station and one was releasing vapour.

The power the cult's leaders had over members was extraordinary. One of the men who allegedly carried Sarin into the metro was a doctor who admits he knew exactly what would happen when he pierced the container with his umbrella. "My heart missed a beat when I received the instructions. I knew the orders to spread the Sarin came from Asahara," said Ikuo Hayashi, a former heart surgeon, in court. He said he had not wanted to release the gas, but feared for the future of the cult and Asahara if he refused. "I am a doctor. I wanted to help people, but instead I killed people. I wish I could turn back the clock," he said.

Other cult members were from equally prominent professions, and at least 60 of their number were serving or former members of the Japanese defence forces. Among them were specialists in tank warfare, helicopter warfare and chemical weapons. Asahara's chief spokesman, Fumihiro Joyu, was a brilliant scientist working with the Japanese space agency before he joined AUM. His handsome features were used to attract young female supporters. Joyu now has a cult following of his own and many fear he will continue AUM's traditions and apocalyptic vision.

There is evidence the cult is re-grouping under the largest body

of supporters in Russia. The CIA told a closed session of the Senate Armed Services Committee that AUM leaders in Russia have recently recruited nuclear scientists and may be trying to build their own atomic bomb at nuclear weapons bases in Siberia.

SO COULD A poison gas attack happen elsewhere in the world? The American Office of Technology Assessment has released a stark warning that a light plane equipped with 100kg of anthrax spores and a crop sprayer could kill more than 3 million people if it flew over Washington DC. Dr Kyle Olson, a chemical weapons expert from TASC, a firm of defence consultants in Virginia, USA, says the public must realise that the threat of bio-terrorism is not a curiosity, but a grim reality as we enter the next century. "A person who is smart, determined, trained in basic microbiological techniques and willing to take a few short-cuts on safety could conceivably do some horrible things."

As society itself becomes more violent, it is perhaps not surprising that terrorists follow suit. They realise that to achieve the dramatic effects they seek, they must move to ever higher rungs on the ladder of escalation. The frequent sights on television of great violence, as well as violent crime, convince them that only extreme actions command TV coverage. And TV coverage is an essential ingredient of a successful terrorist action. Publicity - the so-called CNN effect - is, after all, 'the oxygen' of terrorism.

The history of chemical weapons and their use during and since the First World War generates feelings of horror in most people, and this fear increases their attractiveness as a tool of the terrorist. Their lethality was brought home to the world when Iraq used them against its Kurdish civilians at Halabja in March 1988 where approximately 4,000 Kurds died and 7,000 were injured.

The Western powers have been slow to respond to warnings of chemical weapons proliferation, and the CIA has admitted in a secret report that they "grossly under-estimated" the chemical weapons threat before they saw the reaction among Iranian soldiers of Iraqi use of chemical weapons during the Iran-Iraq war; the CIA reported that soldiers who were prepared to walk through minefields for the good of their country would flee in terror at the prospect of a chemical weapons attack. Chemical weapons: "drove Iran to the negotiating table," according to the CIA.

Inevitably Iraq's 'successful' use of these weapons during the war with Iran encouraged the military in other renegade countries to view them as an 'equaliser', a sort of poor man's nuclear weapon that would put neighbours in their place. For renegade countries also read the larger terrorist group. On January 7, 1989, George Shultz, the then US Secretary of State, told the International Chemical Disarmament Conference in Paris: "Terrorists' access to chemical and biological weapons is a growing threat to the international community. There are no insurmountable technical obstacles that would prevent terrorist groups from using chemical weapons."

Until then, government officials had been reluctant to worry the public about such matters but Shultz decided to break the taboo because the CIA believed Libya could be producing chemical weapons and might supply them to groups like the IRA or an anti-Arafat Palestinian splinter group, as they had with other types of arms.

OF THE THREE types of weapons of mass destruction - chemical, biological, or nuclear - chemical ones are the most accessible to terrorists, as the AUM group dramatically demonstrated. It is easy to find out, from publicly-available literature, how to manufacture chemical-warfare agents and most of the chemicals required to make them are easy to purchase. Anyone with access to the appropriate computer database can find articles in chemistry journals which describe the preparation of, for example, nerve gases. A visit to the chemistry section of a typical public reference library would also produce the same information.

There are five main categories of chemical-warfare agents - incapacitating, choking, blister, blood and nerve agents. Incapacitating

agents are mainly used by police and other forces for riot control. The main effect of these agents - for example, chloracetophenone, or CN - is violent vomiting, induced very rapidly. Choking agents, such as carbonyl chloride or phosgene, attack the respiratory tract making the membranes swell and the lungs fill with fluid so that the victim drowns. Survivors normally suffer from chronic breathing problems.

Blister agents produce large water blisters on exposed skin which heal slowly and may become infected. They may also damage the eyes, blood cells, and respiratory tract. One of the most dangerous blister agents is mustard gas, a persistent agent which can be lethal. It was used by both Iraq and Iran during their war in the 1980s.

Blood agents like hydrogen cyanide and cyanogen chloride are absorbed into the body by breathing, and kill by entering the blood stream and by attacking an enzyme, preventing the synthesis of molecules used by the body as an energy source, causing vital organs to stop functioning.

Nerve agents are in two main groups - the G-agents, which are non-persistent and cause death mainly after inhalation, and the V-agents, which are persistent and can be absorbed through the skin. The most lethal nerve agents are three G-agents - Tabun, Soman, and Sarin (the nerve gas used by the AUM group) - and a V-agent called VX. VX is more persistent and lethal than the G-agents. Of the latter, Soman is much more lethal and rapid in action than Sarin which in turn is more lethal (about three times more) than Tabun.

Nerve gases attack the nervous system and, within minutes of exposure, increasingly severe symptoms appear. They are organophosphorus compounds (sheep dip is one variety) which inactivate an enzyme in the body called acetylcholinesterase which is essential for the normal functioning of the nervous system.

In the body, nerve impulses are transmitted between nerve fibres and various organs and muscles by the compound acetylcholine. When acetylcholine has done its job it is destroyed by acetylcholinesterase, so that the nerve fibres can transmit more impulses.

The nerve gas inhibits the acetylcholinesterase so that it cannot break down the acetylcholine which accumulates and blocks the nerve function.

The symptoms will include contraction of the pupil of the eye, blurred vision, uncontrollable crying, nausea, vomiting, urinary distress, and effects on the consciousness ranging from reduced mental capabilities to convulsions, deep coma, and, finally, death. Death comes from suffocation caused by paralysis of the respiratory muscles. A minute drop of a nerve gas, inhaled or absorbed through the skin or eyes, is enough to kill.

A reasonably competent chemist would have no difficulty in making Tabun, Sarin, and Soman. Tabun (dimethylamido-ethoxyphosphoryl cyanide), a colourless liquid smelling like bitter almonds, is the easiest to make; no particularly special chemical apparatus is needed and it is prepared in two stages. The following formula is widely available and there is no danger in repeating it here. First, dimethylamino-phosphoryl dichloride is prepared from dimethylamine and phosphoryl chloride. Tabun is then prepared from dimethylamino-phosphoryl dichloride and sodium cyanide in the presence of ethyl alcohol. The ingredients - dimethylamine, sodium cyanide, and phosphoryl chloride - can be obtained on the open market.

Sarin (isopropoxy-methylphosphoryl fluoride) is somewhat more difficult to prepare but, as the AUM group showed, it could be well within the capabilities of a terrorist group. It can be made by first preparing dimethyl methylphosphonate by rearranging trimethyl phosphite using methyl iodide. Sarin is then prepared by treating dimethyl methylphosphonate with phosphorus pentachloride and then with sodium fluoride and propyl alcohol.

Having made the nerve agent, terrorists would need to disperse it but only a fraction of a litre would be required to kill a large number of people. Again, the technology for dispersal is not difficult, although the AUM group did not disperse their Sarin effectively. If they had done so, the number of casualties would have been very much greater.

Terrorists could, for example, make or acquire a device to produce an aerosol so that the nerve agent is released as a cloud of droplets. The device could be placed so that the aerosol cloud passes into, say, a city's underground-train tunnel system. If this were done effectively during the rush hour, thousands of people could be killed. Alternatively, the aerosol could be released into the ventilation system of, for example, a large city office block. No Western nation has adequate plans to cope with a chemical weapons attack of this nature, and civilian hospitals would be poorly equipped to handle victims as the Tokyo attack showed.

BIOLOGICAL WARFARE AGENTS are disease-carrying substances and organisms, including bacteria (for example, plague); viruses (such as yellow fever); rickettsiae (like typhus); and fungi (such as coccidioidomycosis). Terrorists could acquire biological agents from civilian or medical research laboratories, or they could culture a biological agent themselves.

The ease with which such weapons can be obtained is shown by the case of Thomas Lewis Lavy, an ordinary 54-year-old American who hanged himself in a prison cell in December 1995 after he was arrested under the Biological Weapons Anti-Terrorism Act of 1989 for possessing Ricin, one of the most toxic substances known to man. Before taking his own life Lavy disclosed he had bought the Ricin in Canada ostensibly to poison coyotes that were killing chickens on his farm in Arkansas.

Such availability of Ricin is deeply worrying: the FBI list it as the third most toxic substance after plutonium and the botulism toxin. There is no antidote and death comes quickly.

Water supplies would be particularly vulnerable to contamination by biological agents. Another likely candidate for terrorist use, as the AUM cult knew, is clostridium botulinum, present in soil. A small sample could be cultured for the large-scale contamination of food, possibly in food-processing factories. Many infected people would become seriously ill and some would certainly die. In October

1996 the Pentagon decided to routinely vaccinate American troops against anthrax, another potential threat.

Genetic engineering has given scientists the capability to produce new biological warfare agents. As more countries acquire biotechnology expertise, the more likely it is that terrorists will acquire such lethal and effective weapons. Scientists can easily identify the genes which determine the lethality of the bacteria that produce diseases such as anthrax and plague. These genes can be spliced into bacteria which are normally harmless. Anthrax, for example, could be put into the bacteria Escherichia Coli, a very prolific bacteria present in the human gut. As a carrier of anthrax, E. Coli could be rapidly produced in large quantities. It would be particularly lethal as the body would be unlikely to produce antibodies, being accustomed to the ordinary E-Coli. Those infected would be unable to fight the disease.

Anthrax is particularly attractive agent for terrorists because it is much more deadly than Sarin, for example, and shows no symptoms for approximately 24 hours, allowing terrorists to release the agent and then escape without fear of detection. It is also relatively easy to turn into a weapon. Kathleen Bailey, a bio-weapons specialist at America's Lawrence Livermore National Laboratory likens the process 'to brewing beer at home'.

THE AUM CULT seduced young scientists into joining their organisation and working on chemical and biological weapons manufacture but there are other means to acquire them. Encouraged by the experience of Thomas Lavy, a terrorist group might use subterfuge to buy the materials or acquire a small stock by theft. Because of this threat, and because of more general fears about the availability of biological and chemical weapons, four senior US senators who have heard expert testimony about the risks, wrote to President Clinton in June 1996 requesting he take emergency action to protect the American people.

"We are talking about a terrorist age where people don't value

human life anymore - this is something we really need to jump on," said Orrin Hatch, the chairman of the Senate Judiciary Committee. "We were startled to learn how easily dangerous pathogenic materials could be obtained and used by individuals who have no legitimate scientific purpose in mind." With Senators Arlen Specter, Dianne Feinstein and Herb Kohl, Hatch called on the President to "implement on a priority basis emergency procedures which will protect the American people against the threat of dangerous, diverted pathogenic materials."

Other warnings have come from army sources. Peter Daly, of the Irish Army Ordnance Corps, who has spoken of the risks posed by chemical weapons, said: "The residue of decades of chemical weapons production still remains to be disposed of and represents an enormous ongoing environmental hazard. For the foreseeable future, the chemical weapon will continue, like the Sword of Damocles, to hang over the head of civilised society. We must plan to address this hazard and to defend ourselves from potential attack, from whatever source."

The larger democracies have proved themselves remarkably reluctant to destroy their own stocks of chemical weapons. In a large advertisement in The New York Times 64 eminent Americans recently told Clinton that getting rid of the "heinous" weapons should be regarded as a priority. Among the signatories was William Colby, former director of the CIA, and eight Nobel laureates. The advert also warned that the AUM attack in Japan could quite easily happen in America.

The main area of chemical weapons leakage is from the former Soviet Union, and there is a serious risk that rogue elements in the Russian armed forces will seek to steal from the vast stocks held in the country. Russia has approximately 40,000 tons of chemical weapons - the largest stockpile in the world, and although the government in Moscow has promised to ensure its safety, many intelligence experts are extremely concerned about the level of security and the danger of 'leakage'. Equally worrying, there is also a risk that chemical weapons which have been secretly developed by smaller nations could be sold to terrorist groups. There is undoubtedly a black-market in these materials. Various attempts to implement a chemical weapons treaty - which would force nations to allow international inspectors access to their most secret chemical stores - have been hindered by the reluctance of some nations to sign and Western intelligence agencies have had huge problems tracking clandestine chemical weapons development which means that sanctions are very difficult to apply.

The former CIA director James Woolsey told the American Senate Foreign Relations Committee recently that: "The chemical weapons problem is so difficult from an intelligence perspective that I cannot state that we have high confidence in our ability to detect non-compliance, especially on a small scale." And yet it is only too clear that countries such as Iran, Iraq and Libya (which have all supplied and sponsored international terrorism) have been assisted by other nations to develop huge stockpiles of chemical weapons.

We know, for example, that the Stasi secret police in the former East Germany trained foreigners, including Iraqis and terrorists, in the use of poison gas. In a television documentary made by Gwynne Roberts, a British TV journalist, a former Stasi instructor disclosed: "There was special emphasis on nerve gases such as mustard gas and Sarin, and also binary chemical weapons. Also discussed were the possibilities of bacterial weapons…anthrax, hepatitis. It was taught how to launch terrorist attacks with chemical means or conventional explosives at airports and train stations. Besides the military training, there was intensive ideological drilling in seeing the enemy only as enemy. And in terms of the enemy, no distinction was made between the civilian population and the military."

At the same time as the secret police were training terrorists and foreign soldiers, other officials from the former East Germany are believed to have helped build chemical weapons plants in Libya and Iraq. The output of such plants was prodigious. For example, a plant at Samarra in Iraq produced up to 700 tons of poison gas every shift. The result is that thousands of tons of chemical weapons have

been stockpiled in smaller nations - a massive threat to global peace and security.

The AUM group 'crossed the line' and used chemical weapons, and it is now clear that society must face the possibility of further attacks similar to the Japanese poisoning. There must be increased international vigilance to prevent the spread of the most virulent chemical and biological weapons to those who have no scruples about using them against innocent people.

Senator Sam Nunn, chairman of the Senate Armed Services Committee has tried to sound the alarm. Recently he warned that terrorists using chemical weapons from the former Soviet Union could attack the US Capitol building with a radio-guided drone aircraft during a presidential address. "They could get in the car one night when the State of the Union message is coming up and from Independence Avenue, launch the drone aircraft and it hits the side of the Capitol building, engulfing that building with chemical weapons and causing tremendous death and destruction and havoc on the leadership of the American government," said Nunn. "That is not farfetched. That is not long-term. That is not new technology. That is all present technology, available technology and hopefully a scenario that will never happen. But nevertheless it could happen."

Governments could make it more difficult for terrorists to make chemical, biological or nuclear weapons by protecting a few key materials. For the manufacture of nerve gases, phosphoryl chloride and dimethylamine should be carefully protected. This protection must take into account the relatively small amounts of these materials needed for terrorist chemical weapons. The biological agents which should be specially protected include anthrax, plague, and botulinum.

To make it more difficult for terrorists to produce nuclear weapons governments must protect plutonium and highly-enriched uranium. The availability of plutonium should be restricted by stopping the separation of plutonium from spent nuclear-power reactor fuel elements by closing down plutonium-reprocessing plants. Most highly-enriched uranium is in nuclear weapons, and when these are dismantled, the highly-enriched uranium should be mixed with natural uranium to convert it into low-enriched uranium, used as fuel in civil nuclear-power reactors but not suitable for the construction of nuclear explosives. However, the most effective counter-terrorism measure is effective intelligence with international co-operation between national agencies.

Chapter Nine

LINKS WITH THE MAFIA

It is ironic that terrorists who claim to be fighting for a 'just cause' are now working in partnership with, or directly supporting, organised criminal gangs. In many cases, terrorism has become nothing more than an elaborate cover for serious international criminal activity, and this is a trend that will escalate during the next decade.

Drug trafficking, the smuggling of weapons, computer-crime and the smuggling of nuclear materials are examples of activities in which both organised criminals and terrorists collaborate. It is extremely difficult to prevent the current high level of criminality that results.

Until recently, organised crime and terrorism were viewed as law and order problems to be dealt with by the individual nation state where the illegal activities took place. Nowadays, however, organised crime and terrorism are increasingly regarded as international problems to be dealt with by co-operation between police and intelligence agencies from various countries.

The development of the global financial market - the operation of which requires the rapid, frequently immediate, transfers of huge sums of money across borders - has changed the environment in which organised crime operates. So has the development of our global transport system, particularly air transport, electronic communication systems and the increase in international trade.

This change of social environment has also led to a fundamental change in the nature of organised crime and terrorism. The new globalism in the post-Cold War world, accompanied by increasing lawlessness and political instability has, not surprisingly, given new opportunities to organised criminal and terrorist groups.

Many leading experts believe that the globalisation of organised crime and terrorism, and the consequent increase in their power and influence, now poses a greater threat to the freedom of democ-

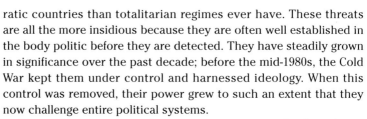

ratic countries than totalitarian regimes ever have. These threats are all the more insidious because they are often well established in the body politic before they are detected. They have steadily grown in significance over the past decade; before the mid-1980s, the Cold War kept them under control and harnessed ideology. When this control was removed, their power grew to such an extent that they now challenge entire political systems.

To tackle this growing threat governments are slowly realising they must allow their law enforcement agencies to co-operate with others elsewhere. European nations have taken this co-operation one step further by establishing Europol, a police force which, while still in an embryonic stage, could ultimately act as a type of 'FBI' across the entire continent. In September 1996, European home affairs ministers met in Dublin and agreed to speed up the ratification of Europol's founding convention, which should now be completed by the end of 1997. The ratification which - in the light of the threat from international crime and terrorism - should have been completed several years ago, will finally allow Europol to become a fully-fledged crime fighting organisation if it wishes.

The meetings took place at the time a huge paedophile case was shaking the entire Belgian nation, and home affairs ministers agreed to give Europol new powers to fight international paedophile gangs and prostitution networks which reach across Europe.

FOR A NUMBER of years, criminal gangs have been spreading their tentacles and empires across countries and continents by forming strategic alliances with one another. The Italian Mafia, Colombian drug cartels, Russian Mafia groups, Chinese Triads, the Israeli Mafia and the American Mafia all have links. Their most senior people now hold regular 'summit meetings' to discuss new 'business ventures'.

What is new is that these groups possess the power and means to destabilise entire nations. Criminal gangs and terrorists are increasingly taking over the functions of some states from Somalia, where the warlords run the shanty towns, to Rio de Janeiro, where drug gangs have taken over the provision of some governmental functions and services. In Peru drug traffickers have paid teachers and local civil servants a monthly salary to augment the inadequate salaries paid by the state, while in Colombia, drug cartels fund social services and pay salaries to buy local co-operation and support.

When considering organised crime many countries face a moral dilemma in that the activity brings them many benefits including jobs, investments, economic growth, improved balance of payments, foreign exchange, and so on. Against these benefits are the costs of organised crime - corruption, violence, social disorder and disruption. Russia is a dramatic example: Mafia groups have strong connections with key elements of the government bureaucracy. They control industries, including arms industries, banks, shops and factories. Today, the entrepreneurial class in Russia consists largely of Mafiosi and there are officially estimated to be more than 3,000 criminal gangs or 'groupirofka'. During the Soviet era, no such class was allowed to evolve although crime was far more of a problem than the Kremlin ever admitted. But when the communist state collapsed, the various Mafia groups were quick to fill the vacuum. In the words of Stephen Handelman, a writer and expert on the Russian Mafia: "Crime in the post-Soviet era is often a continuation of politics by other means."

Once organised crime forms a symbiotic relationship with a government, the direct threats to the state seem to disappear, and the government is then unlikely to move decisively against the organised gangs. A symptom of such inaction is often a rapidly increasing number of unsolved murders, and this has already happened in Russia, where the number of Mafia-related murders is worryingly high. Businessmen, politicians, and journalists are among the victims of these generally unsolved killings.

The goals of organised crime are the maximisation of wealth, influence, and power - and the minimisation of risk. These are, of course the same goals as legitimate business. But in pursuit of their goals organised criminal groups have - quite literally - bought influ-

ence with political parties in a number of countries in an attempt to eventually forge a symbiotic relationship with the government. Professor Peter Lupsha, an expert in global organised crime at the University of New Mexico, Albuquerque, argues that when organised crime gains significant influence over the legislative and judicial systems it becomes a serious threat to democracy. When organised crime evolves to this stage, he explains, "the traditional tools of the state to enforce law will no longer work, for organised crime has become part of the state; a state within a state."

Examples are not hard to find. A case in point is the influence of the Colombian drug cartels over Colombia's legislative and judicial systems. Others are the influence of the Yakuza over political parties in Japan, the power of the Mafia in Russia, and the relationship between the Christian democrats and the Mafia in Italy.

The Russian Mafia groups are most concerning because they are exploiting a country which is in many areas falling to pieces but which remains, at the same time, armed to the teeth with nuclear weapons, advanced conventional weapons and vast stocks of chemical weapons. In late October 1996, governments in the region finally started to accept the links between crime and terrorism at a joint conference in Yerevan, when Interior Ministers from the 11 member countries of the Black Sea Economic Co-operation Organisation met to discuss security issues. The ministers issued a joint statement expressing concern about the growing links between crime and terrorism, and said that the: "struggle against crime, especially against its organised forms, must be regarded as a task of primary importance."

THE LEVEL to which Colombian drug cartels have penetrated the Colombian government is a hotly debated issue. If we listen to the American authorities, such as the Drug Enforcement Agency (DEA), they will say the penetration is as high as it is possible to get. The Colombian President Ernesto Samper has certainly had a tough time explaining claims that he solicited money from cocaine cartels for his election campaign. Despite overwhelming evidence of wrong-doing, Samper was saved for humiliation in June when the Colombian congress voted by 111 to 43 to drop all charges against him, most of which resulted from claims made by Fernando Botero, Samper's former defence minister and campaign manager. From his prison cell, he alleged that the President's election campaign had accepted US $7 million from the Rodriguez brothers, who are senior members of the murderous Cali drug cartel.

Many Colombian judicial investigators did little more than shake their heads when they were told the country's Congress had ordered charges to be dropped. They knew that nearly 30 congress-men were under investigation for links to drugs, a number have already been imprisoned and, of the rest, up to 40 per cent were being paid by the cartels. Many of those have become politicians in the first place at the behest of the drugs barons. The international 'war on drugs' has been a complete failure since it was declared, mainly by the Americans, in 1990, and world-wide drug production has increased by at least 100 per cent.

In Japan, the Yakuza criminal gangs have prospered - almost openly - under the very noses of the authorities. With their bizarre rituals, which include covering their backs in tattoos and removing a section of a finger upon securing membership of a gang, and tradi-tional code of silence, the Yakuza have secured influence at the very highest echelons of government. Author Christopher Symour spent several months trailing and talking to the most senior Yakuza for his book Doing Time in the Japanese Underworld. The book is a fascinating account of an organisation which blurs the edges between the black and official economies. Symour estimates the Yakuza have an annual income of approximately US $50 billion from blackmail, robberies, prostitution and the manipulation of the stock-market.

Many compare the Yakuza to the old Southern European Mafia, and certainly the growth and power of the Italian Mafia since the end of the Second World War has been quite extraordinary, although the authorities have recently inflicted major damage on the organi-

sation. The traditional 'code of silence' has lost its power over Sicilian communities which formed the bedrock of Mafia support but at its height Cosa Nostra. operated as a quasi-terrorist organisation; the population was literally terrified into allowing the rotteness to persist.

The links between crime and politics in Italy offer a warning to other countries where the power of Mafia-type organisations is growing rapidly. It is a short step from being a criminal gang to becoming embroiled in politics, perhaps for self-preservation, and from that point such a group becomes more of a terrorist operation. Killings and bombings become the means of wielding power.

The extent of the Mafia's malign influence over Italian politics by such means has been shown by allegations levelled against Giulio Andreotti, the country's former Prime Minister and leading post-War statesman, who has been accused of consorting with the organisation. Tommaso Buscetta, the most famous Mafia 'supergrass', has testified in an Italian court that a Sicilian politician told him that Mafia bosses could count on Andreotti for help.

Buscetta has also claimed that Salvo Lima, a Sicilian who was in charge of Andreotti's political faction on Sicily, was the 'liaison officer' between Mafia bosses and Andreotti. Lima is unavailable to answer this claim: he was murdered in 1992 by hit-men. "Lima, who called Andreotti 'the Good Uncle', told me how we [meaning the Mafia] could rely on the close relations he had with the senator [Andreotti]," said Buscetta.. Andreotti has claimed that the allegations have been invented by the Mafia in revenge for a crackdown he ordered on organised criminal activity.

In March 1996 after a year-long trial, Giacomo Mancini, a former leader of Italy's now defunct Socialist Party, was sentenced to three and a half years in jail because of his links to organised crime. Mancini, who was 79 at the time of his conviction, was one of Italy's most powerful politicians during the 1970s, when the Socialist Party was sharing power with the Christian Democrats. Another senior politician, Antonio Gava, the Italian interior minister from 1988 to 1991, was sentenced to five years in prison on corruption charges in

May 1996. In a humiliating case, Gava was accused of extorting 300 million lire ($190,000) from construction firms who wanted a contract to rebuild a hospital which collapsed during an earthquake in 1980. Further evidence may come from Giovanni Brusca, the senior lieutenant of the so-called Sicilian 'Boss of Bosses' - Toto Riina, who has been "pouring out evidence" linking senior Italian politicians with the Mafia.

The current campaign against the Italian Mafia began when Judge Giovanni Falcone, the widely-respected head of a special organised crime unit, was assassinated in 1992 by a bomb which exploded under his car as it travelled along a motorway in Palermo. According to one informant, Brusca detonated the bomb. Magistrates in Palermo claim Brusca has personally murdered 30 people and he is also alleged to have been involved in a bombing campaign in 1993 which damaged important and symbolic targets such as the Uffizi gallery in Florence and St John Lateran in Rome.

Brusca's 'defection' to the side of the authorities may well prove to be a defining moment in the battle against the Mafia. For the first time in many decades there is a genuine desire among the political establishment to rid the country of its most dangerous criminal elements - many of whom behaved in a manner indistinguishable from modern terrorists. Further evidence of this fundamental political shift came in May 1996 when Romano Prodi became the new Italian Prime Minister, vowing to destroy the Mafia and its connections with the Italian state.

The Italian experience of serious organised crime is now being replicated within other nations around the world, particularly in the former communist nations of eastern Europe and the former Soviet Union. In Poland, for example, politicians and academics have accused the government of failing to act on clear evidence of links between organised criminal gangs and government officials and politicians. Zbigniew Siemiatkowski, a senior member of the Polish government, admits there are secret connections, and has also said that elements of the police force are in league with the gangs.

With a million reported crimes each year - and many more

ignored by the government statisticians - Poland has a tremendous battle on its hands if it is to prevent itself being subsumed by a tide of criminality. The Polish government has recognised the threat and has called for a determined international "war" on organised criminality which it likens to "a cancerous growth". In mid-October 1996, Eugeniusz Wyzner, the Polish deputy foreign minister, said crime has far greater implications than its most obvious individual effects, and his department have submitted a draft resolution to the United Nations calling for the preparation of an international convention against organised 'transnational' crime. It remains to be seen whether the resolution will be endorsed by other countries equally affected by this cancer.

The United Nations should be concerned because legitimate government forces of law and order in areas of some country's simply do not operate. In other areas, particularly rural areas, the police and military are in control during the day, while terrorists control the areas at night.

ORGANISED CRIMINALS have acquired huge arsenals of sophisticated arms - money is not a problem for them. Professor Lupsha gives the examples of the acquisition by a major Thai drug trafficker of several modern missiles, and a Colombian drug cartel which bought several 230-kilogram aircraft bombs from Nicaragua for use on a rival cartel. The black-market in modern weapons from the ex-Soviet republics is an even bigger problem.

The Russian Mafia, for example, were heavily involved in the supply of weapons and oil to the Serbs during the most violent periods of the war in the former Yugoslavia, despite sanctions imposed by the United Nations. Russian gangs used Cyprus as a base to sell millions of pounds worth of military equipment to the Serbs which had been looted from bases in the former Soviet Union. Oil was also a much needed commodity and at one point 100,000 gallons was flowing into Serbia illegally every day, largely under the control of the Russians.

At the time of this smuggling, one Western intelligence official noted how difficult it was to stop a criminal activity which was actively benefiting countries in dire need of money, such as Russia: "We all know what is going on but we are powerless to stop it because those who should be helping are not. While there is profit, particularly for the poorer countries, there will not be the will to clamp down and they will continue to get away with it."

Other links between arms, crime and terrorism - in its broadest context - were evident from the case of Colonel Oliver 'Olly' North who during Reagan's presidency ran a covert intelligence operatrion from an office in the White House. The operations allegedly helped to finance the Contra guerrillas in the Nicaraguan civil war by using US air bases to facilitate the transportation of drugs; money raised in this way was used to buy weapons. The American security authorities have been linked to other types of drug trafficking: when the CIA were supplying large quantities of arms and money to the Mujaheddin, the production of - and the trade in - opium in Afghanistan escalated. Where the arms trade is involved to any significant extent, links develop between the drug trade, the supply of weapons, terrorism, and government officials, including diplomats and intelligence officers, in a murky and sinister political mish-mash.

THE SCALE OF THE international drugs trade is quite astonishing. Since 1989, world-wide drug production is estimated to have doubled and, according to the US Drug Enforcement Agency (DEA), the area of land used to grow opium increased from 2,400 hectares in 1991 to 20,000 hectares in 1993. In 1989, about 800 tonnes of opium were traded globally; today, 3,000 tonnes are traded, while cocaine production increased from 800 to 2,000 tonnes between 1989 and 1994.

In the face of these staggering statistics, the enforcement agencies can do little to stem the drug tide. A DEA officer graphically summed up the situation: "It is no exaggeration to say that the lead-

ers of these international drug organisations have built powerful financial, transportation, intelligence and communications empires which rival those of many small governments. Few, if any, global industries are as efficient as Narcotics Incorporated."

Some terrorist groups in Latin America who actively describe themselves as 'freedom fighters' are in fact among the continent's major drugs traffickers. One example is the Revolutionary Armed Forces of Colombia (FARC), established 30 years ago as the military wing of the Colombian Communist party. The group, the largest guerrilla force in Colombia, is reported to have about 5,000 active armed fighters and approximately 10,000 supporters. Their aim is ostensibly to overthrow the Colombian government and ruling establishment. To this end, FARC has conducted armed attacks against a variety of targets in Colombia, including the bombing of American businesses, the kidnapping of Colombians and foreigners for ransom, and assassinations.

Some idea of the extent of the link between the drugs trade and terrorism is given by Peter Lupsha. In his words: "Somalia is a case study in organised crime conflict and warlordism in which drug trafficking of Khat [a popular drug] is an intimate part. In Lebanon, the reality of much of the fighting around the 'Green Line' was over drug warehouses and opium and hashish shipments, as well as religious faith and differences.

"The Tamil guerrillas of Sri Lanka have financed their war, at least in part, by trafficking heroin to Europe. The Colombian FARC and ELN guerrillas, like the Burmese Communist Party in Myanmar, have increasingly become drug lords, rather than warlords or revolutionaries. In Peru, Sendero Luninoso's Huallaga Valley front and MRTA are today little more than camp followers and security forces for the drug traffickers.

"In Pakistan, violence and urban anarchy frequently combine organised crime drug and arms trafficking with religion and ethnicity. In El Salvador, street gang criminals deported from the United States have established Los Angeles style gangs, and are forming ties to the major Mexican drug trafficking groups, such as the

Arellana-Felix organisation of Tijuana." Lupsha says the terrorist connection with the drug trade and crime is hardly surprising given the need of every terrorist groups for large sums of money to fund operations.

One organisation which has straddled the ground between terrorism and crime is lead by Khun Sa, a Burmese opium warlord. Khun Sa has been, for many years, one of the most wanted men in the world. He lead an army of 20,000 called the Mong Tai which controlled much of the international heroin trade from the hills of Burma's north-eastern Shan state (CIA estimates say 70 per cent of the world's heroin trade originated from Khun Sa's 'Golden Triangle', which borders Thailand, Burma and Laos). Khun Sa has always claimed he is a freedom-fighter who wants independence for the Shan state, but in reality he is nothing more than a powerful criminal who has used the issue of Shan independence to protect his massive heroin empire. Many intelligence reports suggest the Mong Tai are actually better equipped than the regular Burmese army, and when Khun Sa decided to surrender to Burmese troops at the beginning of 1996 his soldiers handed over a number of advanced surface-to-air missiles and thousands of guns.

In early October 1996, there were reports Khun Sa was operating from a villa in the capital city, Rangoon but these were denied by the Burmese authorities. "He is now under the supervision of our law enforcement officers. He is not doing any sort of business in Rangoon or elsewhere inside our country," said Colonel Kyaw Thein, from the Burmese Defence Ministry.

In Northern Ireland, both loyalist and republican terrorists have been implicated in drug-dealing. According to Ronnie Flanagan, the Deputy Chief Constable of the Royal Ulster Constabulary (RUC), one pound from the sale of each ecstasy tablet sold in the province is probably going towards supporting loyalist paramilitaries, who are "directly" involved in drug dealing. The RUC believes the Provisional IRA is also involved but less directly than the loyalists - instead it is said the PIRA allows, or 'licences', individuals and syndicates to operate at the same time as it is claiming to be avowedly anti-drugs

and inflicting heavy punishments, such as knee-capping, on those it accuses of dealing. The RUC is now indicating, however, that it has noticed PIRA is becoming more involved in the dance rave scene, allowing drugs to be sold alongside alcohol at some of the night-clubs it runs in Northern Ireland.

Chapter Ten

ULTIMATE THREAT

The black-market in weapons of all sorts is so buoyant it is inevitable stories circulate that a number of terrorist groups have been offered nuclear materials and even a nuclear device. Many commentators are also concerned that they might acquire a nuclear weapon by stealing one from a military stockpile or while it was being transported.

These fears have been enhanced by the break up of the former Soviet Union and the economic and social chaos now evident in Russia. But it is not only the fate of ex-Soviet nuclear weapons that we should worry about. As plutonium and highly-enriched uranium become more available world-wide, it is increasingly possible for a sub-national group to steal, or otherwise illegally acquire, fissile material (for civil or military use) and fabricate its own crude but devastating nuclear-explosive device.

These dangers are further compounded by the fact there is so much fissile material, plutonium and highly enriched uranium, in the world which could be used to make nuclear weapons. These materials are ideal for smuggling: a kilogram of weapons-grade plutonium, for example, would be about the size of a golf ball and worth one or two million dollars on the black-market.

It is also difficult to detect. Weapons-grade plutonium and highly-enriched uranium does not always register on radiation monitors because the materials emit very weak radioactivity. With shielding, detection becomes even harder.

According to intelligence sources, a number of former Soviet nuclear weapons are already missing. In the mid-1980s, before the former Soviet Union began to break up, there were about 30,000 nuclear weapons on Soviet territory. The majority of these weapons may still be relatively secure while they are in the hands of the Moscow-controlled military and the security services. In more isolated outposts, given the fact that many Russian troops have not

been paid for months, there must be a significant risk of a device falling into the wrong hands. In September 1996, for example, several Russian soldiers were killed when the warhead of a missile they were probably trying to steal exploded at a military base in Komsomolsk-on-Amur in Russia's far east, approximately 250 miles from its Pacific seaboard.

Concern about the theft of fissile materials has been greatly enhanced by recent Russian smuggling cases. There are dozens of recorded incidents but the world must face the reality of smuggling: only a small percentage of the illicit trade is intercepted.

Phil Williams, an expert on international crime at the University of Pittsburgh, USA, warned in the journal Scientific American, that in almost all illicit markets, only the tip of the iceberg is visible. He went on: "There is no reason why the nuclear-materials black market should be an exception. Police seize at most 40 per cent of the drugs coming into the USA. Law-enforcement officers are less experienced at stopping shipments of uranium than in seizing marijuana or hashish".

It is quite possible that more fissile material has been stolen from the former Soviet Union in the last few years than was produced by American scientists in the first three years of the Manhattan Project to build atomic weapons for the allies during the Second World War. An analysis of some of these thefts and smuggling cases shows just how much more Western governments must do to prevent terrorists, or criminals, from obtaining fissile material and then building their own bomb.

Some these incidents are extremely serious, while others have proved to be little more than elaborate scams perpetrated by Western and Russian criminal gangs. In 1992, a worker at the Luch Scientific Production Association in Podolsk, Russia, stole 3.7 pounds of highly enriched uranium (HEU). The suspected destination of the HEU was never revealed by the Russian authorities who prosecuted the man and clammed up. In November 1993 a Russian Naval Captain managed to steal more than 10 pounds of HEU from a naval base in Murmansk which was used to store submarine fuel.

He planned to sell it on the black-market.

The German authorities have also caught smugglers operating out of Russia. In May 1994 they found 5.6 grams of 'supergrade' plutonium in a garage in Tengen belonging to Adolf Jaekle, a 54-year-old businessman they suspected of running a counterfeiting scam. Jaekle said that his 'customer' was an Iraqi national and Western intelligence agencies were concerned that tests showed the plutonium to contain gallium, used by the military to add extra stability to plutonium in high-yield nuclear device.

By subjecting the plutonium to exhaustive tests, the German authorities discovered evidence it had been produced at the Arzamus-16 nuclear weapons laboratory near Moscow, which was supposed to be one of the most secret and secure sites in the whole of Russia. If there was 'seepage' from Arzamus-16, the entire Soviet nuclear arsenal could be exposed to pilfering. Although the amount in Jaekle's possession was statistically small, the plutonium is highly toxic and could have been used to contaminate water supplies of a major city.

Just one month after Jaekle's arrest, police in the Bavarian town of Landshut secured 0.8 grams (0.028 ounces) of highly enriched uranium during a complex police 'sting' and surveillance operation against smugglers from Munich led by a female estate agent. Five men, a Czech and four Slovaks, were arrested at a motorway service station while carrying 120 uranium pellets in a briefcase and it was clear their origin was the former Soviet Union.

The bulk of highly-enriched uranium in use is military (only about one per cent is civil). There are approximately 1,900 tonnes of highly-enriched uranium in the world - 700 tonnes in the USA; 1,000 tonnes in the former-Soviet Union; roughly 15 tonnes in each of the UK, France and China. Pakistan has probably produced about 150 kilograms of highly-enriched uranium and South Africa about 360 kilograms. Only about 20 tonnes of highly-enriched uranium is used in civil facilities, almost all of it as fuel in civil research reactors.

On average, a nuclear weapon (using an implosion design) contains about 15 kilograms of highly-enriched uranium. The dismantling of nuclear weapons will produce about 30 tonnes of highly-enriched uranium a year in the USA and in Russia.

Another sting at Munich airport in August 1994 uncovered approximately nearly half a kilo of near-weapons-grade plutonium. The plutonium had arrived on a plane from Russia which was also carrying Russia's Deputy Minister for Atomic Power. German intelligence agents were intrigued - even more so when they discovered the plutonium was being smuggled by a Colombian. The man was arrested along with two Spanish men who had been on the same flight. The entire event has come under intense scrutiny after critics said the smugglers had been 'encouraged' to bring the material into Germany by the authorities. However, one German intelligence official defended the sting: "We believe we only captured a small 'taster' of nuclear material that had been sent as a sample - a precursor to a larger shipment of 4 kilograms of weapons-grade plutonium that would be more than enough to make a small nuclear device."

In August 1994 the authorities in Bremen, Germany, seized a sample of plutonium from Russia with an official stamp from the All-Regional Isotope Institute in Moscow still clearly visible.

Left to right -Julio Oroz, 50, of Spain; Justiniano Torres, 38, of Colombia; and Javier Bengoechea, 61, of Spain, sentenced for smuggling a 363-gram pellet of weapons - grade plutonium on a flight from Moscow

Meanwhile, within Russia the authorities were trying to plug more leaks. Reports said that nearly 400 kilograms of weapons-grade uranium was confiscated by security police in Odessa, in the

Ukraine, enough for 20 atom bombs. In August 1994 the KGB arrested three men in Russia who were in the process of attempting to sell 60 kilograms of unspecified nuclear materials.

In December 1994 in Prague, the heart of another former Communist state, three kilograms of highly enriched uranium, worth several million dollars, were captured by police and secret agents. Worryingly, one of the three men detained by the Czech authorities during the operation was a nuclear physicist, the other two were Russians. According to sources within the Czech Interior Ministry the men were in the process of "testing" the material, which had a Russian certificate of origin and authentication.

The authorities had swooped as the men were driving through Prague and the uranium was in metal boxes in plastic bags sitting on the back seat of their car. According to Jan Subrt of the Czech Interior Ministry, the quantity and quality of the material seized was unprecedented, containing almost 90 per cent uranium-235.

Prague was the setting for another seizure in April 1995, when the authorities arrested nine people and confiscated more than 100 pounds of uranium which was found in a car travelling from the Ukraine to Slovakia. The Czech government has said it feels "overwhelmed" by nuclear smuggling and has asked for international assistance in their investigations. "We have no special way of identifying these cargoes," admitted one government official. "With drugs, we have dogs. With radioactive material, we have no technical equipment to use at the border that could identify it and allow us to stop it."

In December 1995, security forces in Kazakhstan discovered nine pounds of uranium in the back of a car they had stopped, while in February 1996 seven armed men were arrested in Lithuania with 220 pounds of uranium. There have been other cases since. Police in the Urals have seized four containers with 198 pounds of radioactive caesium inside.

This smuggling has continued with only occasional successes by the Western and Russian authorities and no apparent let up in the nuclear leaks. As recently as August 1996, five nuclear smug-

glers were arrested by soldiers from an elite 'Alpha' special forces unit of the Belorussian KGB. The 'Alpha' soldiers raided a house in the town of Borisov, near Minsk, just as the gang was preparing to move six containers of 'nuclear materials' (the KGB have not yet fully disclosed what was in the containers) from their hiding-place in the cellar. As this book went to press, the Russian Academy of Sciences was said to be still investigating the source from which the 'nuclear materials' were 'leaked'.

The Turkish secret police are said to have broken-up a smuggling ring supplying nuclear materials to Iran. According to sources within Israeli intelligence the gang was in direct contact with a senior government official in Tehran, and had already received an advance payment for plutonium and other nuclear materials. Mossad, the Israeli intelligence service, is believed to have warned Israeli politicians and the CIA that Iran is now less than two years from developing its own nuclear weapons. This view is supported by evidence from Moscow which suggests that the Kremlin's decision to help Iran with their civil nuclear program will also have military applications. Mossad's concern is that some of the states considered to be Israel's enemy could reprocess and enrich low-grade nuclear material they obtain for civil use to make a warhead. Arms investigators monitoring the activities of the Iraqi military after the end of the Gulf war discovered two of these enrichment programs.

There are also allegations that a political group in South Ossetia, Georgia, a former republic of the old Soviet Union, has acquired what is described by intelligence experts as a 'battlefield nuclear weapon'. The Russian government have admitted that 'something' has gone missing, but they say it is a type of military simulator designed to give their troops a taste of conditions they might encounter on a battlefield during a nuclear war. Mysteriously, they claim the device will explode and produce a mushroom cloud, but say it has no nuclear element.

These and other smuggling incidents can leave the international community in no doubt that an international black-market exists for fissile materials. The Sudanese government has even admitted that

Khartoum airport has been used by a number of government agents and arms dealers to conduct illicit discussions on nuclear deals.

INTO THIS COCKPIT of spies, smuggling and intrigue have stepped international observers and investigative journalists. The Guardian newspaper, London, probed Russia's nuclear industry, and its reporters uncovered one former Soviet nuclear inspector who was far from impressed at the level of security. "They say: everything's marvellous," said Vladimir Kuzetsov. "But what does that mean? I know that in Tomsk-7 there's eight to 10 kilos of plutonium unaccounted for." That is enough to make one crude weapon and perhaps two if the designers knew more advanced techniques.

Not only is there a growth in the level of smuggling (which increased from four cases in 1990 to 241 in 1993), but ever more radioactive material is finding its way on to the black-market. The German Federal Criminal Office, the BKA, has described this increase as a "quantum leap" in quality. A secret leaked report by the German BND intelligence agency for Chancellor Helmut Kohl said this was extremely difficult to control. Sources said that since the BND started tracking the activities of nuclear smugglers, the criminals and terrorists have begun to use alternative routes out of the former Soviet Union, through Turkey which is less aware of the problem and ill-equipped to combat international gangs. There are also well-established smuggling routes from Russia through the Baltic states, Lithuania, Latvia, and Estonia. Another exit point is through Vladivostok to China.

In recent years, according to a British intelligence source, the Russian Mafia has become increasingly involved in this smuggling trade: "The smuggling is unpreventable, unstoppable, and one of the greatest threats to the future security of the West."

A major cause of the leaks is the state of older nuclear facilities in the former Soviet Union. Western visitors to the Kurchatov Institute, a prestigious nuclear research centre, have discovered a worrying lack of security. Founded 50 years ago, it houses seven

A scientist at the infamous Igor Kurchatov Atomic Energy Institute in Moscow stares intently at a small ball of unspecified "radioactive material"

nuclear reactors within its rusty, barbed-wire fences in the middle of a densely populated suburb of Moscow. Kurchatov is one of dozens of institutions in the former Soviet Union that occupy a grey area between the civilian and military sectors. Critics have said that such sites have been ignored when it comes to improving security and simply left to deteriorate.

Nor is it surprising if scientists in such facilities turn a blind eye to theft or actively participate in such crimes. They are under-paid, demoralised and ignored. In 1994, before the nuclear seizure in Bremen, scientists at Arzamas-16, the plant where Western intelligence believe the plutonium was produced, wrote an open letter to President Yeltsin - and anyone else who would listen - complaining their pay had been stopped and they could no longer feed their families let alone live in the style expected by some of the most senior nuclear scientists in the country. Yeltsin, already weighed-down by demands from civil servants, the military and the public for more money and more supplies, could do little to help. When other nuclear industry employees heard of the protest, they also decided to take action and workers at several nuclear power stations went on strike.

There are as many as one million employees of the Russian nuclear industry. Many of the most senior members have travelled abroad, seen the far higher standards in the West and returned disheartened. Many feel they have no choice but to consider alternative sources of income if they are to provide for their families.

THE RISKS may be all too evident but the Russian authorities appear to be blind to them. In an interview with the Russian media before a nuclear-safety summit in Moscow in April 1996, Viktor Mikhaylov, Russia's Minister for Atomic Energy, was asked about nuclear leaks from state plants. He appeared have no concerns. "I would note that installations belonging to Russia's nuclear complex have always had, and still have, a sophisticated and rigorous system of accounting, storage and protection of nuclear weapons and their components, which meets the IAEA requirements and which is constantly being upgraded in the light of the situation as it develops at the facility in question and in the country as a whole," said Mikhaylov. "Russia advocates the expansion of international interaction to prevent the illegal circulation of nuclear materials and the increased mutual exchange of information. An analysis of the information available to the relevant organisations enables the conclusion to be drawn that on Russian territory at the moment there are no organised criminal groupings specialising solely in this area. So far, neither the Russian nor the foreign representatives of the relevant organisations and departments have managed to identify a single real purchaser of nuclear materials. Nor have there been any cases in which the state structures of a 'threshold country' have shown any interest in nuclear materials."

The minister went on: "Russian criminal law has four articles which envisage liability for the unlawful handling of radioactive substances. A special government commission has been created which examines problems pertaining to the nuclear weapons complex. The 'Russian Federation State Targeted Programme for the Creation and Provision of Physical Protection Systems for Installations in the Nuclear Weapons Complex, the Nuclear Industry, Power Engineering and Science of the Russian Federation Ministry of Atomic Energy and Installations of the Russian Defence Ministry' has been elaborated and is being implemented. This programme envisages measures to improve the physical protection of nuclear facilities. Legislative acts have either been adopted or are currently being elaborated to regulate the following the procedure for the

accounting, monitoring, storage and physical protection of nuclear materials and facilities, the handling of nuclear weapons and their components, and ensuring their security during production, storage and transport."

Mikhaylov was probably trying to reassure the Western security agencies and the Pentagon but it is doubtful he succeeded. It is known the security surrounding some of Russia's nuclear institutions would be laughable if what they are guarding was not so serious. The Russian press reported that two teenagers recently clambered through an unlocked window at a secret Moscow nuclear facility and wandered through a sensitive laboratory containing stocks of highly-enriched uranium. No alarms sounded, there was no instant arrest and imprisonment, and no armed guards. It was also reported that alarms at other plants had been switched off by the local electricity company for non-payment of bills.

As already discussed, further intelligence sources contradict Mikhaylov's carefully prepared statement. It is simply impossible for the Russian authorities to guarantee the security of their several hundred nuclear facilities, hundreds of tons of plutonium and up to 1,200 tons of highly enriched uranium contained within. There is still no proper system of checking the number of warheads which, according to a number of senior Soviet officials, are still being counted manually using paper and pen rather than a central computerised registry. This inventory system has obvious failings. Inspectors remove the seals and open up warheads but only to check electronic equipment such as their guidance systems. Several Russian sources have confirmed to me that checks are not made on the presence of radioactive material and it would be relatively easy to steal the contents and replace the seal without discovery.

Western governments, desperate to keep Russia politically stable, are reluctant to criticise President Boris Yeltsin's nuclear policies. The nuclear safety conference held in Moscow in April 1996 turned into little more than a display of international support for Yeltsin in the run-up to national elections, despite explicit warnings from the CIA of the dangers of nuclear leakage. Just a few weeks before the summit, some of the CIA's most senior agents told members of the Senate Armed Services Committee that "the chilling reality is that nuclear materials and technologies are more accessible now than at any other time in history - due primarily to the dissolution of the former Soviet Union and the region's worsening economic conditions."

In March 1996, members of a permanent Senate subcommittee on investigations received a high-level report by Washington's General Accounting Office stating that the detection of nuclear smuggling has so far had more to do with luck than because of any skilled nuclear controls. This view was further supported by Louis Freeh, the head of the FBI, who said there are an increasing number of people selling the material, but the FBI knows: "little about those who are seeking to buy it."

Many experts believe there is little that the West can now do to prevent either nuclear smuggling or another major nuclear accident to rival the one at Chernobyl. Thomas Cochran, director of the nuclear program at the Washington-based Natural Resources Defense Council, believes there was little point in the heads of government who attended the Moscow summit raising the issue of nuclear safety and security. They "would be better served by having a prayer breakfast," he said. "The only thing that stands between us and another nuclear accident is the grace of God."

The West has failed to honour all its promises to help Russia with cash to dismantle its weapons of mass destruction. The US 'Spending on the Co-operative Threat Reduction Program' is costing approximately $300 million, which is only a tenth of one per cent of the total annual US defence budget. The American Department of Energy has been given less than $100 million to provide assistance to the Russians and help them improve nuclear security. It is clear that unless much larger resources are made available, the Russians cannot secure their own facilities.

According to Professor Graham Allison of Harvard University, who was an Assistant Secretary of Defense in 1993-94 and is still retained by the Pentagon as a special advisor to the Defense

Secretary, the Clinton administration's efforts to increase safety and security in the former Soviet Union have been hampered by a lack of co-ordination and funding. Allison said: "In general, the US effort has proceeded at a slow pace and on a small scale. The basic weakness of the Clinton administration's response to the nuclear leakage threat has been the absence of a concerted high-level effort to overcome obstacles." Allison cited Russia's reluctance to accept American help or the need for it, and the ambivalence of Congress and other NATO governments. A report in 1995 for John Gibbons, Clinton's chief science adviser, from a group of leading scientists called for a senior member of the National Security Council to be given overall charge of the US campaign to safeguard Russian nuclear facilities, but it was largely ignored, and the responsibility was distributed among various government departments

One indication of a lack of a nuclear security culture in Russia is the lax methods of the disposing of radioactive waste. Russian nuclear submarines routinely discharge radioactive liquids into the oceans; reactors from decommissioned nuclear-powered submarines are simply dumped into the oceans, as is other radioactive waste; and huge areas around nuclear establishments, civil and military, have been severely contaminated by radioactivity. It is under these conditions that nuclear materials can easily go astray.

In the short term, international help is needed to improve nuclear security by training relevant staff and to assist the authorities to develop and adopt adequate nuclear regulatory oversight. Russia's nuclear regulating body - Gosatomnadzor (GAN), created in December 1991 - is virtually powerless. Unless GAN is given the legal power to improve nuclear safety and security, lax practices are bound to continue.

The evolution of a culture of nuclear security and safety and the establishment of an adequate national regulatory organisation with the power to enforce action against reactor operators and other nuclear establishments will not be easy in a country described by Jonathan Steele, former Moscow correspondent of The Guardian, London, as "a country without law and or a sense of social responsibility among the elite". Other observers have been even less complimentary.

In his interview, Mikhaylov claimed his country knew the whereabouts of all its nuclear materials, but this is also flatly contradicted by an official from the Russian Security Council, who said that more than 10 per cent of Russian nuclear material was officially "hidden" during Communist rule - and the new Russian government did not know where it now was. The Russians have also sought help from the US to track this down without any obvious success.

BOMB-MAKERS with nuclear ambitions, and with access to black-market nuclear materials, would happily opt for an atom bomb far less sophisticated than the types of nuclear weapon demanded by the military. A gun-type nuclear explosive device, using highly-enriched uranium as the fissile material, is the simplest model and this is the design most likely to produce a powerful nuclear explosion. It might have a yield equivalent to several thousand tons of TNT. The problem facing the determined terrorist is that enriched uranium is much harder to acquire than the only alternative - plutonium - and getting that to work is a little more tricky. Both HEU and plutonium will spontaneously explode if enough of the material is brought together so that it weighs more than the 'critical mass'. Getting them to explode and release huge amounts of heat and energy depends on the presence of a very low level of particles called neutrons when the weapon is made to 'go critical' or 'fission'. Highly enriched uranium of the right purity generates a low level of neutrons and an explosion can be achieved simply by slamming together two lumps of HEU of sufficient quantity.

Luis Alvarez, a nuclear-weapon physicist who worked on the Manhattan project, has emphasised the ease of constructing a nuclear explosive with this material: "With modern weapons-grade uranium, the background neutron rate is so low that terrorists, if they have such material, would have a good chance of setting off a high-yield explosion simply by dropping one half of the material

onto the other half. Most people seem unaware that if separated highly-enriched uranium is at hand it's a trivial job to set off a nuclear explosion... even a high school kid can make a bomb in short order".

In practice, two pieces of HEU are brought together by firing one segment into the other. A primitive gun-type design could use a thick-walled cylindrical 'barrel', with an inner diameter of about eight centimetres and a length of about 50 centimetres. A cylindrical mass of highly-enriched uranium, consisting of about 90 per cent uranium-235 and weighing about 15 kilograms, would be placed at the top of the barrel. The larger piece of uranium, weighing about 40 kilograms, would be placed at the bottom, in the firing line. This would be hollowed out so that, when brought together, the smaller mass would fit snugly into the cavity.

To detonate this atom bomb, which is identical in principle to the weapon that destroyed Hiroshima, Japan, in World War II, a high-explosive charge at the top of the barrel would be exploded by a remote-control device. This charge would propel the smaller piece of uranium into the other. The length of such a device is likely to be no more than one metre and about 25cm in diameter. It should weigh no more than 300 or so kilograms - easily transportable by, and detonated in, a van. Such a bomb should explode with a power equivalent to that of a few hundred tonnes of TNT. It might even have a yield of a few thousand tonnes. To put this in context, the largest conventional bomb used in World War II contained about 10 tonnes of TNT; it was christened 'the earthquake bomb'.

A LARGE terrorist group should have little difficulty in building such a weapon, but they might find it easier to acquire civil plutonium, a by-product of reactors generating electricity. The amount available from civil reprocessing plants is rapidly increasing because more capacity is becoming operational. It has to be stored as there are limited civil uses for it which presents an immediate risk of theft, a risk that must be taken very seriously.

The largest conventional bombs used in warfare have had explosive powers equivalent to about 10 tonnes of TNT. The largest terrorist explosion so far has been equivalent to about one tonne of TNT. It is therefore quite obvious that a nuclear explosion equivalent to 100 tonnes of TNT in an urban area would be catastrophic.

If it was exploded on or near the ground such a nuclear explosive would produce a crater, in dry soil or dry soft rock, approximately 30 metres wide. A smaller nuclear explosion (with an explosive power less than a few kilotons) would spread radiation over a larger area than that affected by blast and heat. The area of lethal damage from the blast produced by a 100-tonne nuclear explosion would be roughly 0.4 square kilometres; the lethal area for heat would be about square 0.1 kilometres; and that for radiation would be roughly 1.2 square kilometres.

According to calculations made by Professor J. Rotblat in 1981 anyone out in the open within 600 metres of such an explosion would almost certainly be killed by the direct effects of radiation, blast or heat. Many other deaths would occur, particularly from indirect blast effects such as the collapse of buildings, from falling debris, or from being thrown into objects. Huge numbers of people would be seriously injured and the heat and blast would cause fires from broken gas pipes, petrol in cars, and so on. The area and extent of damage from fires would probably exceed those from the direct effects of heat.

A nuclear explosion at or near ground level would produce a relatively large amount of early radioactive fall-out. Heat from fires would cause radioactive particles to rise into the air; they would then be blown downwind and eventually fall to the ground at rates and distances dependant on wind and weather conditions. The area significantly contaminated with radioactive fall-out, possibly several square kilometres in size, will be uninhabitable until decontaminated, and it would take a long time to decontaminate it to a level sufficiently free of radioactivity to be acceptable to the public.

An explosion of this size, involving many hundreds of deaths and injuries, would paralyse the emergency services; they would find it hard enough just to deal with the dead. There would be considerable delays in releasing injured people trapped in buildings, and many - if not most - of the seriously injured would die from lack of medical care. In the UK, for example, there are only a few hundred burn beds in the whole of the National Health Service. The inevitable panic and hysteria which would accompany any large explosion would also cause huge problems for the emergency services: experience shows that when large explosions occur in an urban area panic also affects the trained emergency personnel. This panic would be considerably enhanced by the radioactive fall-out accompanying the explosion.

Plutonium cannot be made to explode using a gun-type mechanism. A design using the principle of implosion - an inward-directed blast - has to be employed. Terrorists would tend to use a crude version of the atomic bomb which destroyed Nagasaki. The aim is to compress a ball of plutonium (tennis ball size) which is just below the critical mass in normal conditions. As it gets smaller in volume, it gets more dense and therefore goes critical.

A NUCLEAR DEVICE could be constructed using plutonium either in metal form or as plutonium oxide (PuO2). The oxide is a powder and this is the form in which it is normally stored. But converting it into plutonium metal is a straight-forward chemical process.

A small group of people with appropriate skills could design and fabricate a crude nuclear explosive using the metal with very little specialised equipment. Nor would they need access to classified literature. A scientist, Amory B. Lovins, published all the data needed in the scientific journal 'Nature'.

Machine-shop facilities, which could be hired, would be used to shape the material into a sphere. It should be done in a fume cupboard, preferably in an atmosphere of an inert gas, such as argon. While this is certainly not an easy process, it is far from impossible, as demonstrated by two British students, Mike Sweatman and Bob Lowe, who published a pamphlet setting out the scientific requirements for a bomb based only on their own intuition: their research was astonishingly accurate.

The bomb-makers would probably use an amount of plutonium close to the critical mass - in the case of metal, about eight kilograms. This plutonium would be surrounded by conventional high explosive. A number of detonators, perhaps 50 or 60, would be positioned in the explosive making it likely the implosion would be symmetrical which is essential if the plutonium is to be compressed satisfactorily. The aim would be to fire the detonators as simultaneously as possible.

Making an atom bomb using plutonium oxide would be easier

because it is simpler and is safer to handle. The metal can burst into flames in air, as sodium may do. Also, a group is likely to want to avoid the complication of converting it from the oxide. The main disadvantage with plutonium oxide is that the critical mass is much higher - 35 kilograms. The volume of reactor-grade plutonium in the form of plutonium-oxide crystals is about the size of a cabbage.

In a crude nuclear explosive device, the plutonium oxide could be contained in a spherical vessel placed in the centre of a large mass of a conventional high explosive. A number of detonators would be used to set off the explosive, probably by remote control. The shock wave from the explosion could compress the plutonium enough to produce some energy from nuclear fission. The probability of getting a significant amount of fission energy could be maximised by using a neutron counter close to the vessel containing the oxide as it was being poured in. As soon as the neutron counter indicated the presence of neutrons the pouring would be stopped.

The explosive power of the device will depend mainly on how

Some statements made by scientists and politicians have implied that plutonium produced in nuclear-power reactors cannot be used in nuclear weapons. In 1994, for example, Ambassador Ryukichi, the former Japanese Ambassador for Non-Proliferation stated: "Reactor-grade plutonium is of a nature quite different from what goes into the making of weapons...Whatever the details of this plutonium, it is quite unfit to make a bomb".

This statement is totally incorrect. The reality is expressed by Robert Seldon, a nuclear-weapon's expert at Lawrence Livermore Laboratory in America: "All plutonium can be used directly in nuclear explosives. The concept of ....plutonium which is not suitable for explosives is fallacious. A high content of the plutonium 240 isotope (reactor-grade plutonium) is a complication, but not a preventative".

According to Hans Blix, the Director General of the International Atomic Energy Agency: "The Agency considers high burn-up reactor-grade plutonium and in general plutonium of any isotopic composition...to be capable of use in a nuclear explosive device. There is no debate on the matter in the Agency's Department of Safeguards," he said in 1990. That reactor-grade plutonium can be used to fabricate nuclear weapons was proved when the Americans exploded at least one such device during the 1960s.

close to critical the quantity of plutonium oxide gets. With a near critical quantity, a relatively small amount of compression could produce fission energy. Success will depend on the risk the people making the device are prepared to take.

If they get too close to criticality they may be exposed to a strong burst of neutrons, and irradiation by neutrons is a major health hazard. If they overdo it even more the bomb would go off. However that is unlikely to worry an apocalyptic group like AUM in Japan or an Islamic fundamentalist group that believes death in pursuit of a terrorist objective is almost a holy duty.

Again the size of the nuclear explosion from such a crude device is impossible to predict but even if it was only equivalent to a few tens of tonnes of TNT, it would completely devastate the centre of a large city. Such a device would, however, have an excellent chance of exploding with an explosive power of at least 100 tonnes of TNT. A kiloton is not impossible.

PLANTING a crude nuclear device as described would be no more difficult than deploying a large car bomb. A van in which it was hidden could be positioned so that even if it fizzled, and a significant nuclear explosion failed to occur, the explosion of the high explosives would widely disperse the plutonium. Incendiary materials might be mixed with the explosives to create a fierce fire. The plutonium would burn strongly, producing small particles that would be taken up into the atmosphere in the fire-ball and scattered far and wide downwind.

These would be inhaled and embedded in people's lungs, irradiating the surrounding tissue with alpha-particles which are given off when plutonium nuclei undergo radioactive decay. Lung cancer would be the likely result which is why plutonium, when inhaled, has such a high toxicity rate.

The threat of dispersion makes a crude nuclear explosive device using plutonium a particularly attractive weapon for terrorists. The dispersal of many kilograms of plutonium over an area of a city

would make it uninhabitable until it was decontaminated, a procedure which could take many months. The great fear of radioactivity by the general population enhances the threat.

This type of danger is so worrying that the mere possession of significant quantities of plutonium by a terrorist group is a threat in itself. If it proved to a government that it possessed some plutonium, it would be a powerful means of blackmail. The government would not need to be convinced that the group had the expertise to design and construct an effective nuclear explosive device. It would know that even an ineffective nuclear device would cause a huge human catastrophe.

COULD A TERRORIST GROUP actually make a nuclear device or is the previous hypothesis incredible? This question has been addressed by scientists at the Office of Technology Assessment (OTA) of the US Congress. The OTA concluded: "A small group of people, none of whom have ever had access to the classified literature, could possibly design and build a crude nuclear explosive device. They would not necessarily require a great deal of technological equipment or have to undertake any experiments. Only modest machine-shop facilities that could be contracted for without arousing suspicion would be required. The financial resources for the acquisition of necessary equipment on open markets need not exceed a fraction of a million dollars. The group would have to include at a minimum, a person capable of researching and understanding the literature in several fields and a jack-of-all trades technician. There is a clear possibility that a clever and competent group could design and construct a device which would produce a significant nuclear yield (i.e., a yield much greater than the yield of an equal mass of high explosive)".

The question has also been considered by a group of American nuclear-weapon designers who pointed out there would be some potential hazards for the terrorists. Carson Mark, a former American nuclear weapons designer cites the possibility of inadvertently

allowing the bomb to go critical and the toxicity or radiological dangers. But Amory Lovins argues these should not be exaggerated. He shows that the radiation dose rates from plutonium - including reactor-grade plutonium oxide - are such that they would not deter a person from handling it. He concludes that, given sensible precautions against a criticality accident (by using a neutron counter for example), a terrorist group could limit the risk.

The risks are also further reduced as terrorists gain access to professional, scientific and technical skills. Les Aspin, former American Defense Secretary (and a man deeply concerned about the risk of terrorists obtaining atomic bombs) has pointed-out that the power of supercomputers which were originally used by the Allied forces to develop nuclear weapons after the Second World War can now be bought cheaply and easily over the counter in any high-street computer store.

This factor combined with the increasing availability of the fissile materials which can be used to fabricate nuclear explosives; the relatively small amounts of fissile material, particularly plutonium, needed for a nuclear explosive; the availability in open literature of the technical information needed to design a nuclear explosive; and the small number of competent people necessary to build a primitive nuclear explosive are all reasons for extreme concern.

IT CAN be seen that the detonation of a nuclear device is not the only use terrorists could make of radioactive materials. Perhaps most likely is the possibility a terrorist group will acquire plutonium or an equally dangerous substance and simply threaten to contaminate a large urban area with radioactivity.

A radiological weapon produced by a terrorist group would consist of a mixture of high explosive with incendiary material and radioactive isotopes. When the device was set off, it would produce a fierce fire and the radioactivity would go up into the atmosphere with the fireball. It would then scatter downwind, rendering the area beneath uninhabitable until decontaminated. One only has to see the difficulties of coping with Chernobyl to appreciate how costly and time-consuming this would be.

Police records show that some radioisotopes suitable for such a terrorist purpose have been smuggled out of Russia and made available on the black-market. Other than plutonium. examples include strontium-90, with a half-life of 28.8 years, caesium-137, with a half-life of 30.2 years; and cobalt-60, with a half-life of 5.3 years. Half-life is the time it takes for the material to decay to half its radioactive strength.

Strontium is particularly hazardous because, if ingested by humans, it becomes concentrated in bone, and can cause bone cancer. The decontamination of areas contaminated with caesium-137 is particularly difficult because it sticks to surfaces. Cobalt-60 emits gamma rays of high energy and if scattered over an area would produce hazardous radiation levels for a long time.

On December 22, 1995, a leader of the rebellion against the Russians in Chechnya threatened to explode such a radiological bomb - described as a container of radioactive material surrounded by high explosive. To give credibility to the threat, the rebels arranged a demonstration in Moscow for a TV news team. Reporters were sent to a spot in a park frequented by many Muscovites where they found a buried parcel which was later analysed and found to contain a quantity of caesium-137. The rebels have - so far - not carried out their threat.

Radioactive isotopes are widely used in a number of civil applications: in medicine, industry, and agriculture. It is therefore possible for terrorists to illegally acquire some of these radioactive materials to disperse as a terrorist weapon. Although it would require a degree of technical skill, this type of attack is far from unlikely. As already stated, terrorist groups have shown themselves to be relatively sophisticated in recent years. For example the construction of the explosive device that destroyed the PanAm jumbo jet over Lockerbie required considerable expertise, as did the construction of the nerve gas weapon used in the Tokyo underground.

Marvin Cetron, president of Forecasting International, an American 'think-tank' that has produced a definitive study of terrorism for the US Department of Defense, says he has seen evidence that a number of terrorist groups have begun investigating possible techniques to increase the impact of the explosion of a conventional (i.e., non-nuclear) bomb. Cetron believes terrorists are close to perfecting a device containing a normal explosive and radioactive material such as cobalt 60 or caesium, both used by hospitals.

Chapter Eleven

THE FUTURE OF TERRORISM

The future of terrorism is uncertain but, as we have seen, it is deeply threatening. There seems to be little that governments can do to protect their most crucial 'assets' - without which societies cannot operate effectively - from determined bombers. "Most of these assets are sitting ducks," admitted one British intelligence official. "Transport systems, fuel dumps, liquid gas storage sites, centralised computers, major telecommunication centres; they are all extremely vulnerable to sabotage. But what is most worrying - what really has us guessing - is what to do if terrorists target a nuclear power station."

A modern nuclear-power reactor generates about 1,000 million watts of electricity, enough to provide the electrical power needs of a city with a population of about a million people. There are hundreds of such reactors across the world - 437, to be precise - operating in 30 countries. Some nations, however, are more dependent on nuclear power for their electricity supplies than others.

Lithuania, for example, generates about 86 per cent of its electricity by nuclear power; France about 76 per cent; Hungary about 55 per cent; and Bulgaria and Sweden about 46 per cent each. If one or two large nuclear-power reactors are put out of operation in these countries, the consequences would be extremely serious, not only in terms of the possible explosion but also because of the economic effects.

The attractiveness to terrorists of attacking such a target is obvious. A bomb placed in the right position could release large quantities of radioactivity. From the accident at Chernobyl, we know such an incident could scatter radioactive isotopes across vast areas by the wind. We must also remember that an increasing number of spent reactor fuel elements are being stored at nuclear-power reactors. The storage area for these elements, each of which contains a high level of radioactivity, may also be attacked.

Spent fuel elements are stored at the nuclear plant in a pool filled with water located either inside the vessel containing the reactor or outside but close by. At some nuclear-power plants there is an additional facility within the plant boundary but away from the reactors. In addition, liquid high-level radioactive waste is stored in tanks at reprocessing plants where plutonium is removed from spent reactor fuel elements. The sabotage of these tanks by terrorists could release a large amount of radioactivity.

The public are quite naturally terrified of exposure to radiation and this factor increases the attractiveness of an attack for terrorists, as was indicated by the threat by a Chechnyan group to cause radioactive contamination in Russia by exploding a container of radioactive material. An attack on a nuclear-power plant would attract a extensive media publicity, a major aim of almost every terrorist group. Hoping this will never happen is naive.

Fears are being raised that a terrorist group might plant explosives in a reactor in order to release huge doses of radioactivity. The ANC (African National Congress) in South Africa succeeded in blowing up the core of a civil reactor at Koeberg near Cape Town in the early 1980s. The core was blown across the building but, as it was still under construction, there was no nuclear release.

According to Gordon Thompson, a nuclear expert and director of the Institute for Resource and Security Studies in Cambridge, Massachusetts, who has studied this issue, power stations are a prime terrorist target: "There can be no doubt that a successful attack [on a nuclear power plant] can be accomplished by a skilled commando-type military force, or its terrorist equivalent. This force would need technical advice from people who are familiar with the design and operation of nuclear plants. There are thousands of people around the world who possess the necessary knowledge. Plant security systems are not designed to resist determined attacks of this kind, and knowledge about the vulnerabilities of security systems is widely available." At a time when extremist groups with apocalyptic beliefs are growing in number and strength, when terrorists are increasingly attacking high-value targets in industrialised

countries, the vulnerability of nuclear-power plants must be of considerable concern.

In a recent study of the risk of such terrorist attacks on reactors, Thompson gives some disturbing statistics. "September 1981 to September 1982 encompassed 99 incidents in 24 countries. Of these incidents, 63 involved attacks against electricity generation and transmission facilities, mostly in Latin America but also in Canada, Spain, France and South Africa."

There has also been a worrying history of lesser attacks on nuclear plants. Guards at a nearly completed nuclear-power reactor in Lima were overpowered in an assault by 15 armed men; Basque terrorists detonated bombs which damaged a reactor vessel and steam generator, killing two workmen, at a nuclear-power plant under construction in Arminza, Spain; four anti-tank rockets were fired at a Superphenix reactor in Creys-Malville in France. Other examples could be easily given.

Thompson describes a possible scenario. If the main objective is to "make a dramatic threat or take the plant out of production, the attack could be focused on peripheral parts of the plant, such as the switchyard or the condenser cooling water system (cooling towers, cooling water canals connecting the plant to a nearby body of water, etc.). Such an attack could challenge the plant's safety systems (e.g., the emergency diesel generators). Failure of those systems to respond appropriately would then lead to a plant accident. If the main objective is to produce a radioactive release, the attackers will seek to interrupt cooling to the reactor core and/or the spent fuel pool, either by draining the coolant or by interrupting the processes that remove heat from the coolant. At the same time the attackers will presumably breach the reactor containment to maximise the size of the radioactive release.

"The release could begin within minutes or hours after the cooling is interrupted, depending on the scenario. If the attackers have achieved complete control of the plant, they could arrange for the release to occur after they have left the plant. Some reactor types are susceptible to violent power excursions, as occurred at the

Chernobyl plant in 1986."

Such an emergency could cause the reactor core to melt, leading to the release of a huge amount of radioactivity. Terrorists could therefore initiate a massive nuclear disaster. Few planners seem to have considered this possibility and nuclear-power reactors are much more vulnerable than they need to be. To reduce the risk, reactor designs which reduce vulnerability to attack must be developed and immediately implemented. Yet the complacency of the authorities in the face of the risk of a terrorist attack on reactors is staggering given the size and extent of the disaster which could follow.

Another reason for concern is the rise of right-wing extremist groups with apocalyptic beliefs. As long ago as 1988, Bruce Hoffman, of the Department of International Relations at the University of St Andrews, warned: "White supremacist extremists constitute the most likely element . . . to engage in nuclear terrorism." Right-wing extremist groups often attract members with military experience and these people are likely to have the skills and knowledge needed to attack targets like nuclear-power plants. They are also likely to know where to acquire the necessary equipment and materials.

When considering nuclear terrorism, the rise of fundamental religious terrorism (often associated with 'millenarianism'), is also deeply worrying. In Hoffman's words: "The fact that for the religious terrorist, violence inevitably assumes a transcendent purpose and therefore becomes a sacramental or divine duty, arguably results in a significant loosening of the constraints on the commission of mass murder."

Future terrorists will not be affected by the political and moral constraints which have limited the level of violence used in the past, a fact many weapons experts are now openly admitting: Dr Alastair Hay, a leading chemical pathologist has said: "Everybody involved in chemical warfare has always recognised the risk from terrorism, but it is something that nobody has wanted to talk about openly, simply becuase it might give people ideas." However, as Hay admits: "The genie came out of the bottle with Tokyo."

The Future of Terrorism

Secular terrorists may continue operating on the maxim 'kill one, frighten thousands' but mass killing may fit well with the apocalyptic visions of religious terrorists. Similarly, white supremacist groups, in their war with a central government, may decide to opt for killing on a grand scale. In my view, this is the greatest future terrorist risk.

Perhaps terrorists may also serve another function. Bruce Hoffman argues that terrorists may be employed by countries either to steal nuclear weapons or strategic material from another country, or they may be paid to stage a covert nuclear, chemical, or biological attack to conceal the complicity of a state patron: "In the future, terrorists may become the 'ultimate fifth column', a clandestine, cost-effective force used to wage war covertly against more powerful rivals or to subvert neighbouring countries or hostile regimes."

THERE IS very little understanding among political leaders of the danger that terrorists will acquire nuclear weapons or will acquire fissile materials and fabricate them. Consequently, little is being done to reduce the risk. There are two main problems.

Firstly, there are huge amounts of plutonium and highly-enriched uranium, the materials from which nuclear explosives can be made. The Rand Corporation conducted a study recently for the Pentagon and concluded there is enough plutonium in the world to make 87,000 small nuclear bombs. Secondly, the authorities cannot accurately determine the amount of plutonium in the reprocessing plants, used to remove plutonium from spent reactor fuel elements. The nuclear industry wants to mix surplus plutonium with uranium and use the mixture to fuel nuclear-power reactors, an additional danger. The world's total stocks of plutonium, civilian and military, is about 1,500 tonnes and there are about 1,900 tonnes of highly enriched uranium in the world. Techniques are not sufficiently sensitive to ensure that the diversion of an amount sufficient for the fabrication of a nuclear weapon would be detected.

But this has nothing to do with inefficiency or incompetence. Even using the best available and foreseeable safeguards, technologies and accountancy techniques, the safeguards on reprocessing plants are only about 97 per cent (some say 95 per cent) effective. This means that in a typical reprocessing plant, handling about 7,000 kilograms of plutonium a year, about 200 kilograms are unaccounted for. An operator of the reprocessing plant therefore cannot say for sure whether or not the 200 kilograms of plutonium unaccounted for has been stolen. Only about ten kilograms of plutonium metal are needed to make a nuclear explosive device. This amount would, therefore, be enough to make about 20 atom bombs a year. Six large (commercial-scale) reprocessing plants are currently operating: two at Sellafield, England; three at La Hague, France; one at Chelyabinsk, Russia; and one at Tokai-Mura, Japan. A Japanese plant, at Rokkasho-Mura, is scheduled to start operating soon after the year 2000. Governments should decide the reprocessing of spent nuclear-reactor fuel elements must be stopped. The spent fuel elements can then be placed in permanent storage in deep shafts.

The spent fuel elements are so radioactive they are self-policing: exposure to the radiation from them would be lethal and they must be handled with special remote-handling equipment. Unless commercial plutonium reprocessing is stopped, it must be assumed terrorists will acquire and use nuclear explosive devices. The risk is simply not worth taking for the sake of using plutonium as reactor fuel, particularly because it is, to say the least, extremely doubtful whether there is a financial advantage in using plutonium as reactor fuel.

LET US consider the parlous condition of the state which holds the key to the spread of weapons of mass destruction. The former Soviet Union seems to be sliding inexorably towards total anarchy and, as detailed earlier in this book, criminal gangs are taking over many of the functions of authority. One of the most worrying manifestations of this collapse is the situation within the Russian armed forces, illustrated by the tragic case of Lieutenant Khoruzhev, a deputy commander of the 242nd motorised infantry regiment of Russia's 8th Guards corps. Khoruzhev returned home to his family recently and shot himself dead in front of his wife and young daughter. According to many within the Russian army, Khoruzhev's case is typical: dozens of servicemen are committing suicide rather than tolerating the abject poverty forced upon them by the Russian government, which has failed to pay many for more than six months. Suicides among Russian military officers rose by 28 per cent during 1996, and the figure among lower ranks is thought to be even higher.

Is it surprising that junior officers - who officially receive a pittance of perhaps US $120 per month, but who are not now even receiving those meagre sums - are thought to be responsible for much of the trade in international nuclear material? Even soldiers serving on the front in Chechnya have not been paid and other military forces have no money for food - many units receive just one meal a day. General Igor Rodionov, Russia's defence minister, has acknowledged the threat posed by a simple lack of cash. In November 1996, he warned that the armed forces were in such chaos that the stability of 'Mother Russia' itself could not be guaranteed. This dire state has arisen largely because of massive tax evasion by private and state companies which has caused the state's coffers to shrink by approximately US $7 billion.

The abject human misery that results from this economic failure is seen in Khoruzhev's last day alive. The young lieutenant had not been paid for several months, and his landlord was threatening to evict him and his family from the ridiculously small room they rented. One of Khoruzhev's last actions was to steal half a loaf of bread for his daughter, who was suffering from constant illness and fits of fainting because of extreme hunger.

But it is not only the military who are suffering in the new post-Communist Russia. Vladimir Nechai, the director of the top-secret Russian nuclear weapons research centre Chelyabinsk-70, committed suicide in late October 1996, apparently in despair at the lack of

funds available for his institute.

According to Vladislav Nikitin, Nechai's deputy, workers at the institute had not been paid for nearly six months: "We have sent letters to the President, to parliament, to [Prime Minister] Chernomyrdin, but there has been no reply." Nikitin said that financial conditions were getting worse at Chelyabinsk-70, and that is likely to be the situation in other Russian nuclear research centres. Many were established well away from other centres of population, solely for top-secret research with no other sources of revenue or funding. Now that state funding has been suspended, one can only guess at the conditions in which some of the most brilliant minds in Russia are being forced to live.

In the words of one senior official, scientists and engineers are "making off with whatever they can sell... just to survive." That large quantities of plutonium-239 and uranium-235 have "disappeared" from a plant in war-torn Chechnya beggars belief. I also understand that 800 cubic metres of radioactive material, including unknown quantities of strontium-90 and caesium-137, have recently disappeared from a Russian factory near Tolstoy-Yurt, a village north of Grozny, the Chechen capital.

We cannot turn to the Russian government for accurate answers. It cannot even say how many soldiers are in its army or how many nuclear weapons it owns. Mikhail Yegorov, former head of the organised crime department of the Russian Ministry of Internal Affairs, has recently embarrassed his bosses by warning that organised criminal groups were attempting to infiltrate Russian nuclear installations to steal nuclear materials. He said the same methods used by the Russian Mafia to smuggle precious metals and materials out of Russia have probably been used to smuggle nuclear material.

This contrasts with the comments of Viktor Mikhaylov, Russia's Minister for Atomic Energy, who we quoted earlier in this book, making the claim that Russia's nuclear stockpiles were secure and no leakage had occurred. He must have seen a Kremlin document that has come to light which states there has been a serious "disappearance" and an "unsanctioned removal" of radioactive materials from nuclear storage facilities. The document bears the official stamp of the office of Viktor Chernomyrdin, the Russian Prime Minister, and his office has not denied its provenance. There seems little doubt they ended-up with either a renegade state such as Iraq or Libya, or with a large terrorist organisation.

THESE CONCERNS are supported by a recent internal report passed to me by an American intelligence official and written by the Nuclear Black Market Task Force, a group of officials from the intelligence and defence community who advise the most senior American politicians on nuclear proliferation. It is chaired by Sarah A. Mullen, the Director of the Intelligence, Technology and Analysis Division at the Arms Control and Disarmament Agency. Other members include James Woolsey, former director of the Central Intelligence Agency and officials from the FBI, Department of State and the Senate Permanent Subcommittee on Investigations. Their report makes worrying reading.

"The probability of a nuclear weapon or a bomb quantity of weapons-grade materials from the FSU [former Soviet Union] is growing. The Task Force is particularly concerned that a desperate, corrupt, or coerced official with authorized access could steal warheads or materials or broker a theft," said the report. Despite the number of arrests already made on charges of nuclear smuggling, the Task Force warns that: "...thieves cleverer than those caught in Europe and Russia may have already stolen nuclear weapons or weapons-grade materials and transported them out of the FSU, eluding both intelligence and law enforcement agencies."

The Task Force believes that the "insider threat" from serving Russian officials or military officers still far exceeds the "outsider threat", but it says the danger of an elite military unit entering the FSU and stealing a nuclear warhead must be considered. "Accountability procedures and other defenses against the insider are weak or weakening at the same time that new factors are compromising human reliability: collapse of the internal security

system, severe fiscal constraints, breakdown in military discipline and morale, poverty and institutional corruption (which is pervasive). These increase both the probability of insider theft and such a theft's success."

According to the Task Force, the likelihood of theft of nuclear materials is outpacing improvements in protection: "Materials security in the FSU is poor at best, particularly at civilian research institutes, fuel production facilities and naval fuel sites where weapons-usable materials sometimes are present. These facilities are numerous, remote and controlled by different entities who have mixed reactions to Western assistance efforts. Moreover, several seizures of materials, that had been stolen months before and hidden away while the thieves awaited an opportunity for sale, suggest that some materials are already beyond Western-assisted efforts to improve materials security in the FSU."

The report also tackles the extreme threat posed by such groups as the AUM cult: "Technical requirements suggest that traditional terrorist groups are more likely to use a conventional explosive or other means to disperse stolen radioactive materials than to improvise a nuclear explosive device using stolen weapons-usable materials. By contrast, anarcho-terrorists (such as the Aum Shinrikyo) or a technically sophisticated extortionist group might be less daunted by technical difficulties or political (sponsor) disincentives."

Terrorists of the sort that attacked the World Trade Center in 1993, blew up the Federal Building in Oklahoma City in 1995, or released Sarin gas in Tokyo's subway in 1995 "might acquire a nuclear device or quantity of nuclear material. Indeed, the Japanese cult responsible for the subway attacks was also studying uranium enrichment and laser technology, potential steps to acquiring nuclear weapons, and it had at least one follower on the staff of Russia's Kurchatov Institute, a nuclear physics laboratory."

The Task Force reported that Iranian agents have scoured the FSU searching for nuclear materials, technologies and scientists, although their level of success or failure is unclear: "Iran unsuccess-

fully approached a plant in Kazakhstan in 1992 for a substantial quantity of enriched uranium. Rensselaer Lee, president of Global Advisory Services Inc., cites a 1991 letter faxed to Russia's Arzamas-16 nuclear research center, purportedly from the Islamic Jihad, offering to buy a nuclear weapon and he quotes the center's director as saying Iraqi representatives in 1993 offered $2 billion for a warhead."

So what action do the Task Force propose taking to safeguard Western security? Apart from calling from international summit meetings to discuss the problem, the Task Force suggest that nuclear smuggling should be defined as a "crime against peace",

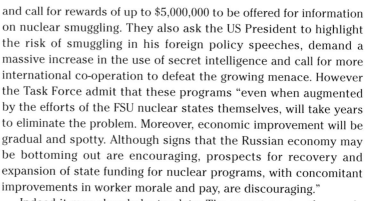

and call for rewards of up to $5,000,000 to be offered for information on nuclear smuggling. They also ask the US President to highlight the risk of smuggling in his foreign policy speeches, demand a massive increase in the use of secret intelligence and call for more international co-operation to defeat the growing menace. However the Task Force admit that these programs "even when augmented by the efforts of the FSU nuclear states themselves, will take years to eliminate the problem. Moreover, economic improvement will be gradual and spotty. Although signs that the Russian economy may be bottoming out are encouraging, prospects for recovery and expansion of state funding for nuclear programs, with concomitant improvements in worker morale and pay, are discouraging."

Indeed it may already be too late. The report quotes the words of a Russian military prosecutor who investigated the disappearance of fuel rods from a Russian naval base in Murmansk: "Everyone in the fleet knew about the poor state of repair of the alarm system on the [fuel rod] store-room... officers and specialists had submitted written reports on this... but the answer was always the same: no money... even potatoes are sometimes better protected nowadays than radioactive materials..." The warnings are now too urgent for governments to ignore. But as we have seen on countless occasions, that is precisely what they are most likely to do unless and until there is an actual attack, explosion or war.

APART from more frequent terrorism by religious fundamentalists (particularly Islamic extremists and Christian white supremacists) and millenarian groups, the consequences of a number of new global socio-economic problems are likely to cause terrorism to flourish in the next few decades. The widening gap between rich and poor countries is already increasing tension between the North and South to such an extent that some commentators speculate it may soon be greater than East-West tension was during the worst days of the Cold War.

Environmental degradation, the debt and bio-diversity crises,

global climate changes and deforestation are among the problems exacerbating this friction. Mounting pressures on non-renewable resources - fertile land, fish, and particularly water - are increasingly recognised as major causes of conflict between Third World countries. But many of the world's problems also arise from population increases. According to demographers, the population of our planet will probably increase from today's 5.3 billion to about 11 billion by the year 2030. The vast bulk of this increase will occur in the Third World, and most of it will go into cities, creating huge 'megatropolises' with populations of many tens, and even hundreds of millions of people.

Most of the inhabitants of these mega-cities will live in abject poverty in shanty towns with inadequate access to medical services, clean water, food, clothing, and housing. They will have woefully inadequate supplies of energy and poor basic education services. These are the classic conditions in which urban violence and terrorism flourish. In the next century, the Earth will almost certainly be unable to cope with such huge numbers of people, and unless drastic steps are taken soon, a reaction through a rising tide of terrorism is inevitable.

So what can be done? Nations should adopt policies to ameliorate the adverse consequences of population growth and our scientific and technical skills should be mobilised to deal with global problems. The problems created by the population explosion and poverty could be solved, or at least greatly reduced, by appropriate technology. Unfortunately the resources needed to apply our scientific and technical skills to solving these problems are often tied up by the military: about 60 million people are absorbed in military and military-related activities and almost all would be better employed in humanitarian research. The figures are simple to understand: the world's research scientists and engineers total about 2.5 million and of these about 500,000 work only on military research and development (R & D). If only research physicists and engineers (those at the forefront of technological innovation) are included, over 50 per cent are working for the mili-

tary, improving existing weapons and developing new ones. Funds given to military R & D currently run at about $80 billion a year world-wide.

The weapons industry, the second biggest business in the world after oil, is being kept going by the military-industrial complex, not for reasons of national security but purely for profit. The skills now monopolised by military science could be diverted to solve many of the problems which face the world as we move into the new millennium - otherwise these problems will simply get worse. The quality of life for most people, both in the developed and in the developing countries, will steadily deteriorate and those in developing countries must expect terrorist attacks to become increasingly frequent and more violent.

As we have seen, the terrorist of the 21st Century is unlikely to be as restrained in their violence as today's. Similarly, tomorrow's Third World terrorists, driven to desperation by the effects of the ever-widening North-South poverty gap and by the increasing lack of social justice it causes, may feel they can only begin to redress the balance by indiscriminate terrorist attacks on the North. We will only escape this fate if political leaders make sure that resources are diverted to solve our serious global problems. But leaders will only act if public opinion is behind them insisting that the adverse effects of over-population and poverty are tackled, and recent history shows us this is extremely unlikely to happen.

Instead, the overwhelming evidence is that we face a new breed of 'revenge-terrorist' emanating from both the Third World and from within developed countries who has no moral restrictions on the use of weapons of mass destruction. As the new millennium approaches, the world must be on its guard to prevent a terrorist group from obtaining nuclear or bio-chemical weapons and producing its own Armageddon.

Instruments of Terror

Index

Index